GROW YOUR
PEOPLE
GROW YOUR
SALES

A leader's guide to creating
a Growth Mindset Culture

LEIGH ASHTON

R^ethink

First published in Great Britain in 2021
by Rethink Press (www.rethinkpress.com)

This book is dedicated to the sales professionals that I've worked with and those I've yet to meet and share a journey with. Your role is so important to the future of our world. Nothing happens without sales.

I hope the ideas in this book help you broaden your sales leadership and create happier and healthier Sales Growth Mindset Cultures that generate more success for you, your team and your customers.

Thank you.

Salvo

I hope this book inspires new thoughts and actions on your development journey.

Leigh :)

Contents

Foreword

Worsening levels of mental health and general wellbeing are being reported across most industrialised nations. Clearly this is impacting the workplace in terms of productivity, performance – and bottom lines. All business functions are affected. But for those in sales and other customer-facing roles, this is magnified. There's no hiding place in sales. If the salesperson 'doesn't feel up to it', sales undoubtedly suffer. A negative mindset cycle begins. . . which is quickly embedded.

Any wellbeing and mindset issues among salespeople land fairly and squarely in the lap of the sales leader and it is the sales leader who is expected to create a highly motivated team, a team where everyone is expected to excel daily and a team expected to block out any inner

stuff that could get in the way of the smashing
of targets.

It's no surprise then that many leaders have their
own mindset and wellbeing challenges, alongside the
added responsibility of being out there, fronting a team
requiring and looking for strategy, direction, coaching,
support and inspiration. Yet what an opportunity you
have. . . being a sales leader is a true gift. To be able to
create, develop, nurture and help a team of salespeople
succeed in their role, and in their lives, can be one of the
most rewarding and fulfilling experiences in business.

Having been CEO of First Direct, Mercury Communications
and Egg Banking, I can vouch for the positive influence
a leader could have with their team; such is the
importance of the role of leader of any size team and in
any organisation. Although the importance of mindset
at work wasn't quite the hot topic that it is becoming
today, creating a healthy and thriving culture with a happy
workforce was always an extremely high priority and a key
factor in the success of every company I have built.

And so, it was a real thrill to meet Leigh in 2011 and
learn about her work in the area of sales mindset and the
role it plays in generating happier and more successful
sales teams and, in particular, her work with sales
leaders.

I've seen the impact her work has had on sales teams
and leaders – taking underperforming sales teams and

supporting them through a journey that leads them from mediocrity to outright winners, and mainly through transforming their mindset and more specifically their sales mindset. It's clear that sales leaders who develop long-term positive changes in their own approach and mindset create the gateway to bring about a happier, more successful sales team.

This book brilliantly captures Leigh's work to date – threading together over 35 years of selling, leading, coaching, training – and always absorbing the latest research and thinking. The result is a blueprint which any sales leader wishing to develop a strong mindset culture can use to drive success in today's fast-evolving business environment.

Every sales leader will love Leigh's 10–80–10 model. This is a great tool for assessing exactly where your individual salespeople are . . . and how you can tailor your leadership to create the perfect development journey for each person. This emphasis on personal growth ensures long-term sales success for each individual. . . and the wider team.

Crucially – and bringing me back to my opening lines of this foreword – this book is exactly what is required by sales leaders in this age where we have to match the need to be kinder and more mindful with our sales teams while ensuring they succeed in what remains a very competitive environment. This book accelerates the journey.

Every company needs to succeed, which means every sales team must succeed. We all want that, but how you get there is important. For me this book sees off the old ways of sales leadership and provides a gateway to a new and more effective way.

Mike Harris
Former founding CEO of FirstDirect, CEO of Mercury Communications, founding CEO of Egg Banking plc, and co-founder of cyber security pioneer, Garlik; currently chairman of Kynd, Dashly and Token.com

Introduction

If you're checking out this book you probably have a desire to improve yourself as a sales leader. You may be way down the path . . . or this could be your first step. What's important is that you want to be a better sales leader. Welcome to *Grow Your People, Grow Your Sales*.

From the moment I started in sales in 1985 I realised I had landed exactly where I was meant to be. I honestly felt that I was being paid to chat with customers and sort their problems every day, which didn't seem like a job at all. I loved it. As a result, I was good at it. . . and so my reward was to be promoted to sales manager. After the initial euphoria of being promoted, I realised this new role was a whole lot harder. Every day since, I have strived to be a better version of myself by learning, applying and sharing. It's not an easy path but it's been truly rewarding and fulfilling.

In my early days as a sales leader, I consumed everything I could to develop my knowledge and skills. I realised pretty quickly that how salespeople think has the biggest impact on their sales success. It's less about developing sales skills and more about personal development; less about instructing and more about coaching; and less about numbers and more about people. I learned that my own mindset and that of every person in my team had the most significant impact on the level of success we could achieve together.

This discovery changed the trajectory of my life. Mindset development became my passion. . . and still is.

The transformations I've seen in people when they shift their thinking to a more positive and empowering mindset have been breath-taking. Struggling salespeople become top performers in a matter of weeks. People settling for comfort over growth suddenly find the confidence to show what they really have inside them. . . and are then promoted. Teams becoming more collaborative and winning bigger deals. Teams caring, sharing and supporting each other in ways the organisation would never have imagined possible, gaining greater happiness and fulfilment.

It's been heart opening, humbling and inspiring.

Every person in your team has extraordinary potential and your role is to create an environment where they feel safe to allow that potential to unfold and to do what salespeople do best: change the future of businesses and lives.

Think of every salesperson in your team as an athlete. Unless they are fit both in skills and mindset, they are not going to be as successful as they could be. There are salespeople that think in a way that means their beliefs and actions drive them toward success. In my experience these people will make up around 10% of your team. They will either naturally have, or have made the choice to develop, a Growth Mindset. More on this later.

The remainder of your team are unlikely to think in this way naturally. That's where you come in. Your challenge, if you choose to accept it, is to develop the Growth Mindset of every member of your sales team. To create a culture of psychological safety where all are inspired to push beyond where they currently are.

This book shares everything I have tested, evaluated and found to be successful tools for shifting the mindset and culture of sales teams. Some activities are super easy and you'll wonder why you haven't already implemented them, some take time and practice to master – but they all work. I've shared these mindset approaches globally and they have the same positive impact regardless of industry or culture. Why? Because they are based on your interactions with the people in your team, a very human interaction. They are all about human development and how you care for the wellbeing and development of each person in your team.

That doesn't mean giving them an easy ride – far from it. It's about regularly nudging them gently into their growth zone and then supporting them through the challenges of personal growth and success. This is great for them, great for you and great for your customers.

If that sounds exciting to you, you're in the right place.

Ready? Let's get started.

What do you want to get from this book?

It's important to focus your mind on your objectives when undertaking any activity. This book needs to be useful to you or there's no point in taking the time to read it. Having a focus in mind while you read will ensure you are primed and ready to embrace the concepts that will help you achieve what you're striving for.

- What do you want to achieve as a result of reading this book?

- What would need to happen for this book to have a big and positive impact on your sales leadership and on the development of your team?

- What are the three most important things you want to achieve as a sales leader?

To help you get the most from this book and apply your learnings, download the accompanying Sales Leadership Journal where you can record all of your responses, insights and actions as you work your way through the book: www.sales-consultancy.com/book-resources

1

What Makes A Great Sales Leader?

This is an important question to ponder. There are many qualities I observe in great sales leaders around the world that light up and inspire their team. These qualities are varied, a special combination that each sales leader has created to suit their personality and the personalities in their team. A combination that develops and inspires each person in their team to be more, do more and show up as the best version of themselves. It's an approach that creates a healthy culture and generates consistently strong sales results.

I can't give you a one-size-fits-all winning formula, but I will share with you the traits that I see over and over again making a huge contribution to sustainable long-term success.

To start with, great sales leaders never focus purely on KPIs and numbers. Instead, they focus on:

- Aligning to a mission that goes way beyond themselves

- Developing and deepening their understanding of how mindset and wellbeing impact performance

- Shining a light on the dark areas of each team member so that they discover and learn through experience

- Creating a healthy Sales Growth Mindset Culture that incorporates psychological safety

- Shifting their leadership style to suit each person in their team

- Coaching rather than telling

- Having 'Tough Love' conversations as soon as they observe the need for them

- Getting to know and understand each person in their team, what makes them tick and what's important to them inside and outside of their work

- Aligning to strong, ethical leadership and development values

- Ensuring each person in the team feels valued and confident to show up as a better version of themselves every single day

This list is by no means exhaustive, but the more of these you adopt, the more effective a sales leader you will be. If you're already incorporating some of these in your leadership, you're on your way. If you're not, this is a great opportunity. Anything you implement from this book is bound to have a positive impact.

Whether or not you realise it, you have incredible influence on your team. It may not feel like it at times, especially if you're not having the kind of impact you'd like. Think of your sales leadership as a shining light – wherever you direct your light, your team will follow. . . normally unconsciously.

Let me give you an example. You're feeling the strain because you're not on track to achieve your targets this month or quarter. Your boss is giving you a hard time. You become a bit grumpy and fed up with some poor performers. Your light and mind are focused on these under-performers and the last conversation you had with your boss. You think you're hiding your negative emotions but your energy contaminates your communication with every person in your team, even those who are performing well. Your team pick up on this and they start feeling negative too, everyone's energy and performance diminishes.

That's the power and impact you have. If you don't manage your issues, you transmit them.

Think of each person in your sales team as an athlete. They need to master their skills (in our case, sales and communication) and mindset to be the best version of themselves. Once a salesperson has learned the sales process, your role is to continually develop their Growth Mindset so that they can use their skills with ease and grace, becoming a master of their craft. You are developing masters of sales and human connection. It's a big responsibility.

I'm often struck by the many similarities between sales leadership and parenting. You are preparing human beings for the next stage of their life journey, developing their skills and mindset to help them become a better version of themselves under your leadership.

Read that again and really take it in.

It's not about focusing on the numbers, it's about developing the people who will bring in the numbers. The numbers are the result of great thinking, good actions and a desire to keep growing. Don't make the same mistakes as so many of the sales leaders that have gone before you. Don't focus solely on the numbers. Develop each salesperson's mindset and the numbers will follow.

The old ways of sales leadership are obsolete and simply don't work in the twenty-first century. Instilling fear in your salespeople and whipping them to bring in more, more, more creates an unhealthy, toxic culture. For those who stay, it leads to burnout, and the talented will leave for greener, healthier pastures. It's a lose-lose.

It's also important to bear in mind that developing your sales leadership using the approach outlined in this book doesn't mean that your entire team will become top performers. A reality check here: each person in your team will be at a different stage of development – you'll have some salespeople on chapter three of their life book and some on chapter thirty. You'll need to determine the specific approach needed to get each person to their next chapter. If you make the mistake of comparing Salesperson A, who is at chapter six, with Salesperson B, who is at chapter twenty-six, at best you will perceive Salesperson A as an under-performer and at worst you'll squash their self-belief, perhaps leading to their demise and subsequent departure from the business – and maybe even sales altogether.

Every person in your team is unique and you'll need all your detective skills to gather the facts of their personality, character traits, values and drivers. And that's not enough. It's also important that you take an interest in them personally. Are they in a relationship? Do they have children, pets, hobbies? Where do they go on holiday? The more you know about them in and out of work, the easier you will find it to lead and develop them.

Another reality check: *your role is not your title, or an entitlement.* You will be judged by your actions and the way you treat and develop each person. You need to get the first demon out of the way – your ego.

We all have an ego. It's not about getting rid of it all together, because it has some positives that keep you striving. It's more about not letting it control your choices, because your ego often makes poor decisions: it tends to choose what is right for your ego rather than what supports the greater good.

You'll know when your ego is at play because your emotions will be playing havoc with your mind. You are likely to be feeling anger, guilt, shame, hurt. . . the list is long. When you notice you are feeling negative emotions, don't make any decisions. Go for a walk or run, wait twenty-four hours, write a letter to the person involved or to yourself. This letter is not to be sent, you can burn or bury it afterwards, it's just to get the thoughts out of your head. If the emotions are still there, keep writing and discarding each letter until you feel neutral. Do whatever you need to get yourself grounded in the reality of the situation and to calm your nervous system. Only then can you make good decisions.

Another demon I need to mention early on is your desire to tell your team what they should or should not be doing. This 'telling' style of leadership is a definite no-no. Why? Because you are training your team to do what you say rather than think for themselves. You are training them to think that you have all the answers and they do not. You are training them not to do something until they've run it past you. If you have a team that is constantly checking in with you about how to do X, Y or Z, that's a strong clue that you are a telling leader. Telling leadership is ego-driven and makes you feel valuable and needed, which may be nice for you but is hopelessly ineffective in developing a high-performing team.

The next time one of your team asks you what they should do, try my favourite response:

'I've got some ideas, but what do you think?'

Then stay silent and let them respond. This won't be easy if you love to jump in and fix things but it will be worth the effort. Usually, your team members know what they should do and you'll be pleasantly surprised when they share their thoughts. If they are on the right track, or thereabouts, I normally say:

'That sounds like a plan – let me know how it goes.'

If they are way off track, it's normally because they haven't taken something important into consideration. Your job is then to shine a light on that darkness by asking a question that exposes their oversight without making them feel small, so that they can tweak their plan. Something like:

'What would happen if. . .?'

Then stay silent, let them ponder and tweak. Even if their plan isn't the best, they will be 100% committed and motivated to make it work because it's *their* plan.

That gives it way more chance of success than anything you might suggest.

If it's going well, they are likely to tell you – make sure you check in with them regularly if they don't mention it, not to interfere but to listen and help them come up with their own changes and improvements.

Awareness of your impact

It's so easy to do or say something without realising the impact you have on the people around you. For example, if you send a group email addressing a negative behaviour from a few people that you're frustrated with, how do you think that will impact on those who aren't displaying that behaviour? Especially those who are exhibiting the behaviour you wish all your team would adopt.

Getting a positive outcome in leadership is crucial. Use this seven-step process to keep you on track in your actions and communications:

1. **Think** about the impact you want before taking any action.

2. **Assess** your inner state – are there any negative emotions coursing through your veins?

3. **Shift** into neutral and detach yourself from any negative emotions.

4. **Establish** the best outcome for all concerned.

5. **Consider** the people involved – how do you need to communicate so that they will hear you?

6. **Take action** and observe the impact of your communication to ensure it's being received in a way that achieves your desired outcome.

7. **Change** what you are doing if it's not working.

This process will help you have calm conversations and meaningful discussions. This is best for you, best for your team and best for the business.

Focusing on creating a positive reaction to your communications going forward will create a positive internal state in each of your team. Why is this important? Because your salespeople can't show up as their best selves and deliver the sales you both want if they are feeling rubbish on the inside. Similarly, you can't do your best work as a sales leader if you feel rubbish on the inside. It's essential you find a way of dealing with your internal negative emotions so that you don't transmit these to your team. You're after a peak mental state that empowers people to go beyond where they are now.

A *Harvard Business Review* study found that happy salespeople generate 37% more sales.[1] Upset your team and you upset your sales. It's important to add here that keeping your team in a positive state doesn't mean

---

1   S Achor, *'The Happiness Dividend', Harvard Business Review* (2011), https://hbr.org/2011/06/the-happiness-dividend

letting them have everything their way or giving them an easy ride. Far from it. You still have to focus on their growth and personal development, which can lead to some stress for them and for you. Nudging people out of their Comfort Zone is a constant challenge. Having those tricky conversations to increase someone's awareness of their poor behaviours is not easy. You have to do these things, and do them with respect and care so that by the end of the conversation they feel good about it too. We'll talk more about this in Chapters 7 and 8.

In order to have a greater awareness of my impact on others, I've developed my ability to observe myself in situations from an observer position, so that I can evaluate my behaviour and give myself feedback. In doing this, I ask myself:

- How do I rate my actions against achieving the desired outcome?

- How would I feel if I was on the receiving end of my communication?

- What impact am I having on the person or people around me?

- Are my emotions or ego getting in the way of the best path for all?

- What would my peers think if they were observing me right now?

- What could I do better?

When observing and evaluating yourself, you have to be totally objective and detached from the you that you're observing. Think of yourself as someone you don't know or someone that you want to develop who has asked you for feedback to improve their approach.

If you're emotionally attached to the you that you're observing, your ego will tell you exactly what you want to hear:

- 'You were absolutely right to get angry.'

- 'Anyone in your position would have shouted.'

- 'That person is an idiot.'

Get the picture? You can't trust your ego in a challenging situation, it will always justify any negative actions.

I've developed this discipline over many years, so I'm able to do this in the moment. You may be applying elements of this already and only need some refinements to get you all the way there. If it's not something you already do, the easiest way to start is to use the questions as part of a review process after an interaction. Take notes on the changes you need to implement to make your next interaction better. Over time, you'll notice yourself asking these questions in the moment, allowing you to observe and evaluate yourself while having these conversations. This is a great skill to master, both for your sales leadership and for your life in general.

Integrity in sales leadership

Integrity is something you feel. It's important not to mistake personal integrity with leadership integrity – you can have the former without the latter. When you have leadership integrity, your team will see it and feel it.

Leadership integrity is about being fair, non-judgemental and non-biased – someone your team can trust. Being honest, respectful, supportive and consistent with every member of your team, not just the ones you like. You may like to add to my list of leadership qualities that demonstrate integrity, but don't remove any – these qualities are all crucial for leading a high-performing sales team. Lack of these qualities and being seen as lacking integrity will have a strong impact on the way your team perceive you, and ultimately on how they perform.

Talking of perception, how do you think your team currently perceive you based on your behaviours in the last six months? It's something worth pondering and, while you do so, keep in mind that far more than what you say to your team, it's your behaviours and how you made them feel that they will remember. What you *say* may not be what you *do*. Kind words with harsh actions will still have a harsh impact.

If you ask your team how they perceive you, your integrity and your impact, they are unlikely to be honest – you are their boss, after all. So, who could you ask?

Is there anyone who would be honest enough to tell you? If you are lucky enough to have such a person, ask them and listen to what they say without interrupting, without judgement or justification. They are giving you a massive gift. Be grateful and thank them. If you haven't got anyone you can ask, you will have to be your own counsel and use the observer questions in the previous section.

You could also ask someone to observe you in action with the specific task of giving you feedback on the impact you have on others, being careful to note responses that indicate a negative impact. These might be sideway glances, eye-rolling, becoming disengaged, or 'Yes, but' language – things like that.

The more you focus on creating a positive impact, the better your sales leadership will become and the more sales your team will generate. Why? Because you will have created a culture of trust, support and growth for all – and that can only lead to good things.

There's a mantra I share on all my Growth Mindset programmes:

'Never compare yourself to others. . . only to the you of yesterday.'

By all means, be inspired by others, but comparing yourself only leads to negative emotions. Remember, you could be comparing chapter ten in your book of life to their chapter twenty-five.

You are not in competition with anyone else, only with the you of yesterday. Are you better than yesterday? Even if it's only by a little bit, you're still going in the right direction. Daily marginal gains are the most consistent path to self-development. At the end of each day, ask yourself:

> 'What could I do differently tomorrow to be a better sales leader?'

Your responses will ensure that you are continually developing and upping your leadership game.

Your development

What do you need in order to show up as the best version of yourself?

You may or may not know the answer, but one thing is for sure – your development is crucial to the success of your team, so make time for it. It starts with making a commitment to yourself. How much are you willing to bend and flex your routine to make time for your development, to be a better sales leader?

Humans are creatures of habit and that means we are easily drawn back to our old default settings unless we commit to change. What do you do when you want to create time for new, better habits?

This is what works for me:

- I write my new actions on post-it notes and put them all over the place.

- I schedule time in my calendar.

- I use an accountability buddy.

- I use a coach.

- I read books, listen to audio books and podcasts, and watch videos on the subject.

- I attend workshops.

- I find easy ways to make improvements.

I can't tell you what will work best for you because we're all different, but I hope my suggestions will help you come up with your own perfect solutions. Consistency is vital. It's much better to do a little every day than allocate two hours a week. Even if you can only do five minutes a day, that's a start. The frequency and repetition create momentum and the new neural pathways you'll need to cement your new habits.

I'll close this chapter with another mantra:

> 'Care more about improving yourself than proving yourself.'

TAKE ACTION

As we come to the close of the first chapter, it's time to think about what actions you're going to take as a result of what you've read so far. They need to be actions that improve your sales leadership skills for the benefit of your team.

Go for the quick wins to start with – it's always good to feel like a winner in the early days, to build your muscles for the more challenging stuff to come.

As your first action, download the accompanying Sales Leadership Journal where you can record all your responses, insights and actions as you work through the book: www.sales-consultancy.com/book-resources

2
The Importance Of Having A Sales Leadership Mission

When you wake up in the morning, what is it that gets you out of bed committed to being your best self for the day ahead? If you know the answer, great – write it in your journal. If you haven't got an answer, it's time to put some effort into creating something. Why? Because without a personal sales leadership mission you are likely to fall into the trap of adopting the corporate version, which is unlikely to be the best fit and is probably very uninspiring. It's possible that yours is great, but most are awful.

Let me clarify what it is I'm asking you to do. A sales leadership mission is something that inspires you to be the best version of yourself. You don't have to share it if you don't want to, it's just for you.

Some pointers to consider when creating yours:

- Keep it to one to two sentences max.

- Make it memorable – you must be able to repeat it in your mind without looking.

- It should inspire you.

- Focus on what's best for your team, so they too can show up as their best selves.

- Ensure it fills your heart with joy, pride and other positive emotions.

- Create a statement that keeps you moving in the right direction, making the right choices for you and your team.

- Check that it has a positive impact on your salespeople, your customers and your sales.

- Avoid corporate speak. It must come from *you* and be in language you would use. Remember, this is just for you – you don't need to impress anyone.

It may take you a few iterations to get there, but you have to start somewhere. Go and grab a coffee, find a quiet space where you won't be disturbed, switch your phone off, make some notes, doodle, do whatever it is you do when you're creating ideas. Use the list of pointers above, but let yourself sit in silence if nothing flows immediately. I know that can be tough – us sales pros love noise, but it will be worth it if you give it some time.

Think about twelve months' time from now – who and where do you want to be? If you need some inspiration, go to my website (www.sales-consultancy. com/book-resources) where I share some personal sales leadership missions of the many sales leaders I've worked with. If there's something there that is the perfect fit for you, try it on for size for a week or two and tweak it where necessary to make it fully yours.

Once you have it, make a note of your sales leadership mission in your journal. To give you the best chance of making this mission a habit, repeat your sales leadership mission on waking, before going to sleep and throughout the day. It needs to become your North Star, guiding your actions and decisions.

Now that you have your personal sales leadership mission, it's time to turn your focus to your team.

The 10–80–10 rule

Over my many years of working with sales teams, I've noticed that a 10–80–10 ratio shows up time and time again. This manifests as roughly 10% of a team who are top performers. These people are amazing regardless of the quality of leadership in place, because they rarely need it. They are going to perform well no matter what. Not only do they achieve, they also do it in an ethical way that's aligned to the corporate values. These guys are generally outcome focused, with a Growth Mindset. We'll talk more about the Growth Mindset in Chapter 5.

Then, roughly 10% of the team will be under-performers. No matter what you do to help them, it never quite works out. There are all sorts of reasons for this – their heart isn't in the job, a lack of self-belief or of confidence, or they are lost in what I call the 'Valley of Reasons and Excuses'. It can be one or more of these reasons, but these team members usually have a Fixed Mindset.

Then there's roughly 80% of the team who sit in the middle. Some months are good, some are poor; some may hit their target but don't go far beyond it, even though they could with a bit more effort.

Your biggest wins are with your 80% salespeople. They want to do it. They can see the top performers above them and want to be like them. They tend to fluctuate between a Growth and a Fixed Mindset. This causes them to either avoid new approaches for fear of failure or humiliation or, when they are brave enough to try, they do so apprehensively, meaning they generally get a mediocre result and so pull back and feel reluctant to try again.

They are the ones that really need your support to step out of their Comfort Zone. Coaching them every step of the way so that they don't go running back to safety is the surest way to develop them to greatness. The more you focus and support this slice of your sales team, the greater the sales increases you'll get.

Were you a top 10% salesperson?

If you were, this can make it harder for you to have empathy with the other 90% of your team. You might struggle to understand why they just don't get on with it and simply do the things that create results. 'What is the matter with these salespeople?' you might frustratedly ask. That's what I did too. I come across this situation all too often in sales leadership. I hear things like, 'They are just lazy, useless, a waste of space, incompetent, not fit for purpose. . .'

Yet, when the sales leaders I work with realise that not everyone is like them and some people simply need a helping hand, a leader who believes in them and someone they can turn to when they are having a tough time, they suddenly see the potential. Once they change their approach they start to see a shift in thinking within the 80%, and better results follow. Not all of those salespeople will become top performers but they will all do more than they are doing now. How would you like an extra 10% from each of these salespeople? How about 20%? Some will even double their sales when they get the support they need to get through the fog of fear and negativity.

Just to be clear, being supportive doesn't mean being nice all the time. You need to push and challenge your team beyond what is comfortable and make them uncomfortable. This is when they'll need you most – not to make it easy, but to give them the confidence to take each step. Taking one step after another. . . knowing that you're there supporting their growth and development. Done well, these experiences and conversations will be the things they remember most about working in your team, and remember with fondness.

The first step is to identify who your 80% salespeople are, the people you want to focus on developing. Your 10% top performers just need a quick check in, some positive reinforcement, then you can leave them to do what they do best – generate sales. Your 10% under-performers need to decide for themselves whether they are committed to making it happen. You can support them, of course, but you can't save them – they have to choose to save themselves.

In my early years of sales leadership, I made the mistake of trying to save my under-performers because I wanted them to succeed. In doing so I simply delayed the inevitable, which was painful for me and stressful for them. The best thing for everyone is to help them find a role that lights them up, that inspires them to be their best self and, if you can help them to discover what that role is, then you've done a great thing. Remember: saving someone is not the same as supporting them. Do the right thing, not the easy thing.

The Five Keys to Sales Leadership Success

When you observe any successful sales leader, you'll notice that there's no single personality type that stands out as the 'successful type', they come in all forms. This is great news and means you don't have to conform to a specific personality to be a successful sales leader.

There are, however, some things that every successful sales leader has in common. They are all excellent at:

1. Being totally clear on what they want to achieve.

2. Taking action to achieve their desired outcome, even when they aren't 100% sure what the right action is.

3. Noticing what works and what doesn't in the achievement of their goal.

4. Changing what doesn't work and testing new options.

5. Having rapport within themselves as well as everyone involved in achieving the goal.

If you can develop these five abilities, you will be an even better sales leader. Let's look at each of them in turn.

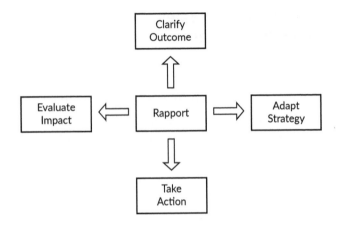

The Five Keys to Sales Leadership Success

Be clear about what you want to achieve

Of course you want to achieve the team targets and your KPIs for success, but how do you want to get there? Are you going to drive your team to the point of exhaustion? Do you plan to shout at them until they surrender and do things exactly as you want them done? Hopefully, you want a happy and motivated team full of self-belief and confidence to do what it takes to achieve their KPIs and sales targets. Whatever it is you want, get totally clear on how you want to show up and what impact you want to have as a sales leader and as a sales team.

Take action

Once your outcome is established, you need to decide on the first step towards it. This first step creates momentum and gives you valuable feedback that can guide the next step. You don't need to be fully confident in the entire journey – just the first step. Confidence grows with each step.

What actions do you need to take to enable your sales team to deliver your identified outcome? Coaching, supporting, developing, mentoring – the list of skills you will need to draw on is long, and each member of the team will need a unique approach to suit their needs.

In the process of developing your salespeople you will need to stop telling and start asking them how they think they can contribute to the outcome. Give them feedback – this should be positive and developmental. Get comfortable with letting them make mistakes sometimes, as this is the best way for them to learn and grow. In later chapters, we'll take a deeper dive into the skills you will need to do this.

Constantly evaluate

This one is simple. Is what you are doing with each person working, or not? Assess your progress at every opportunity, don't wait until the end to evaluate. Deviate from your plan if it isn't working. The bottom line is: if something is working, keep doing it; if it isn't, stop.

If what you are doing isn't working, adapt and do something else

Just because something works in one context, doesn't mean it will work in every context. It's the same with your team; an approach will work for some and not others. If something isn't working with someone, change your approach and keep evaluating the impact until you start to see progress toward your chosen outcome.

Rapport, rapport, rapport

You must have strong connections with every individual in your team and with any other people involved in the success of your outcome. You must care about them and fully believe in their ability to succeed. You also need rapport to inspire them to greater heights, to go that extra mile.

Think about yourself, too. Are you 'in rapport' with yourself? Do you really want this? If you're in conflict with yourself, this will manifest initially in discomfort and evolve into resistance and reluctance. In this downward spiral it's impossible to do things well because part of you is only doing it because it's required, and another part of you doesn't want to do it at all. You can't give it your all because all of you doesn't want to do it.

How can you lead your team with 100% integrity when you're not fully on board? You can't. The success of your sales team starts with you, so you must bring together the parts of yourself that are at odds with each other.

Let me share a real example from a sales leader I worked with. Part of them knew they needed to have a conversation with one of their team who was exhibiting behaviours that violated core values. They were a top performer who got highly emotional whenever approached about their less than perfect behaviour; it would take them days to get over it. The team were heading towards the end of the quarter and a bit off target. The sales leader needed their salespeople firing on all cylinders to ensure the best chance of hitting target. However, his inner conflict about the problematic behaviour of that one team member was adding to his stress levels and he was aware that other members of the sales team were observing him do nothing about the situation.

If this was you, what would you do? Think about it before you read on – your response will tell you a lot about yourself. Would you focus on chasing the target, or would you have the difficult conversation and risk impacting that salesperson's performance?

In this example, the best solution – and the one the sales leader took – was to have the conversation. Yes, the person was a top performer but he was one person and his behaviour was negatively impacting the whole team. When the rest of the team saw that the issue had been addressed, they all worked like crazy to achieve their target. Not only that, eventually the sales leader had to fire the person in question because his behaviour did not improve. The sales team collectively generated far more sales going forward, which more than made up for the exit of their top performer. People who violate values have a negative impact on others – be sure to keep on top of it. Remember: don't do the easy thing, do the right thing.

Sometimes the conflict is within you. Maybe you feel a bit awkward with one of your team because you raised your voice at them. You know it wasn't your finest moment and feel bad about it. You want to apologise but you feel it would be a sign of weakness. The solution? Get over yourself. Don't let a moment like that get in the way of your rapport with every member of your team. It's simple – just apologise.

Remember the Five Keys to Sales Leadership Success:

1. Be clear about what you want to achieve with your team

2. Take action

3. Constantly evaluate how you are doing

4. If what you are doing isn't working. . . adapt and do something else

5. Rapport, rapport, rapport

You can also use the Five Keys to assess the impact afterwards. The following questions will help guide you:

1. Were you clear about the outcome you wanted?

2. What action did you take?

3. What was the impact of your action?

4. What other approaches did you try to increase your positive impact?

5. How strong was your rapport with the person/people involved?

These questions will help you identify the areas where you need to strengthen your approach and improve your overall success rate for you and the team.

TAKE ACTION

It's time to think about what actions you're going to take as a result of reading Chapter 2.

For the best results, work on your sales leadership mission, and review the 10–80–10 Rule in relation to your team. Actions should follow the Five Keys to Sales Leadership Success outlined in this chapter to improve your skills for the benefit of your team, so focus on outcome, action, impact, different approaches, and rapport. Again, you should aim for some quick wins to start with – this is a great way to build your muscles for what comes next.

3
The Mindset Challenge

How do you influence your salespeople to grow and evolve every day in all areas of their lives, so that they can show up as the best version of themselves? You can't do it unless you get under their skin. What's important to each member of your team? What lights up their life? What inspires them to be more? What makes them get out of bed each day motivated to be their best?

You need to be curious and ask questions. Take your time – don't be inspired to try and find out everything about someone in one conversation, they'll feel like you're interrogating them or trying to steal their identity. This isn't a task to tick off, it's a relationship-building process. It's similar to what you would do with a potential customer, finding out about them so that you can help them achieve their goals. Use a similar 'gently does it' approach. Treat each of your team as you would a client and you'll be about right.

Understanding what's below the surface of each individual gives you a better idea of the landscape of your salespeople. You'll discover their psychological preferences and how you need to take these into account to influence and support their growth. You must also accept that your psychological preferences will need to take a backseat if you are to help and influence your team.

Of course, there are psychometric tests you can use, but these don't tell you that Pete is married to Sue, has three children – Rema, Shyma and Xander – one in primary school, one in secondary school and one at college. They don't tell you that they have three dogs named Mindy, Ziggy and Domino, that Mindy came from Battersea Dogs and Cats Home and Domino was one of her pups that they didn't know about when they brought her home. You need to know so much about people to be a great sales leader, this isn't simply about work.

Again, think of salespeople like athletes – they need to be in the best state of mind to perform. It's a useful analogy to keep front of mind. You have to use a holistic approach with salespeople, as you would with athletes. Processes and structures will only get them so far, it's what goes on in their heads that makes the biggest difference to their performance, which is why you need to know and understand what's in there. Only then can you decide on the best approach to get them from A to B.

In this chapter I'm going to share some mindset hacks that you can use, first for yourself so that you fully understand the team members, and then with your team.

TFAR

I'm starting with this mindset hack because it's so easy, and potentially life-changing. It can be used in any context – sales, career, health, money or family. You name it, this will have a positive impact. That's true for everything I share in this book; these concepts can be applied in all areas of your life and I strongly encourage you to do so. The more you use them, the easier they will become, generally leading to greater happiness and success.

If you've not come across the concept of TFAR before, this psychological tool – which has been adopted and adapted in many areas of self-development – helps show us how our thoughts impact on results, as follows:

Your **Thoughts** generate your **Feelings**, which influence the **Actions** you choose to take, and these deliver the **Result** you get.

$$T \Rightarrow F \Rightarrow A \Rightarrow R$$

Everything that happens in your life, every result, is triggered by a thought. It's unlikely that you are consciously aware of that thought because it will be so deep rooted that it occurs without your full awareness. But while you may not be consciously aware of your trigger thought, you will always be able to detect what you are feeling. Is it comfort, excitement, anticipation or some other positive feeling? Or is it fear, discomfort, anxiety or some other negative feeling? Why does this matter, for you and for your team?

For you

I'm going to take you through a short exercise so that you can experience this phenomenon for yourself, then I'll share with you how to use it with your salespeople.

EXERCISE: TFAR Part One

Find yourself a quiet corner where you won't be disturbed. Switch your phone off and give the exercise your full attention. Ready?

Think about something that you love to do, that you know you're good at. It can be something you do as a sales leader or something more personal, but it must be something specific that you can focus on. It needn't be a complex thing. Maybe you make the best veggie curry, are a brilliant gamer or a great brother or sister.

Once you have a specific activity in mind that you love to do and know you're good at, I want you to imagine that you're just about to do it. What feelings do you notice in your body? Give yourself a few moments to connect with this feeling.

Having used this exercise for many years, I know that the feelings you experience will be positive, because of the context of what you're thinking about. The kinds of responses that people share include anticipation, confidence, happiness, calm and many other positive feelings.

Now you may not always know what the exact trigger thought was that created the positive feeling but you can be certain that the positive feeling in your body can only have been triggered by a positive thought, because that's how the mind works. A negative thought would not trigger a positive feeling, and vice versa.

When you have a positive thought combined with a positive feeling, every cell of your body is going in the same direction and you become 100% laser focused on your commitment to whatever the associated action might be. When you are fully committed in this way, your action will deliver an amazing result. This reinforces your trigger thought and creates a loop of positivity. You'll consistently repeat your success, over and over.

Hopefully you're feeling happy right now in your loop of positivity, but I need you to clear your mind for the next part of the exercise.

EXERCISE: TFAR Part Two

I now want you to think about something that you don't like to do. Something that makes you feel a bit uncomfortable. It could be a sales leadership activity, such as having a tricky conversation with one of your team, or your boss. It should be something that you don't like doing and that you know is not your best skill. If you can't think of a sales leadership activity, look to other areas of your life for a specific example. A highly specific example will mean you get the most out of this exercise.

Ready? Now think about doing that thing that you really don't like doing and know you're not great at. What feeling do you notice in your body? The kinds of responses I hear when I do this exercise with clients include 'anxious', 'worried', 'fear', 'a big knot in the stomach' and other negative feelings. What are you feeling?

You'll know from what I explained earlier that a negative feeling can only be created by a negative trigger thought. This is likely to be something along the lines of, 'I really don't want to do this', 'I'll humiliate myself if anybody sees', or 'Why do I have to keep doing this?'

When part of you doesn't want to do something, but another part of you knows that you need to, your energy becomes fragmented. Some of your energy is going towards the activity and some is pulling away. Your energy starts to polarise and it becomes a dance – a couple of steps towards the action you need to take, then three steps back. You are doing the cha cha cha but you don't even want to be on the dancefloor.

When you have this much tension in your body, it's impossible to take laser-focused actions. This means you can't show up as your best self and so you won't get the result you want, reinforcing your negative trigger thought and creating a loop of negativity. If you continue in this loop of negativity you will come up with a million different reasons not to take the action you need to take – maybe you already have areas like this in your life.

Fortunately, there is a simple hack to resolve this issue. The next time you feel a negative feeling arising before starting an activity, stop. Do not continue with the activity – it will be pointless and stressful, a waste of energy.

Instead, take a couple of deep breaths and consider what your trigger thought might be. . . guessing is fine.

Write it down.

In every situation there are many perspectives. Your trigger thought is just one. You've chosen it because of a previous negative experience you've had. Think about the situation at hand and walk around it in your mind. What can you see from different perspectives? What alternative trigger thoughts could you choose instead? Come up with five or six alternative perspectives. Here are some examples I've heard from clients to get you started:

- 'Every time I do this, I improve my approach.'

- 'This is another opportunity to practise my skills in the Learning Zone.'

- 'Each time I do this, I get the feedback I need to become great at it.'

- 'The more I do this, the easier it feels and the better I get.'

- 'The more I practise, the faster I will master this.'

Get the picture? Once you have your five or six alternative trigger thoughts, try them on for impact. Say each one to yourself, in your head or out loud, and notice what feeling it generates in your body. Pick the one that resonates with you most and creates a positive feeling in your body. Then, the next time you do the activity, repeat this to yourself over and over.

You may not immediately create a super positive feeling that has you racing towards the activity with 100% enthusiasm. Not yet anyway. But you will have something that's aligned with hope, anticipation and relaxed feelings that enable you to take that laser-focused action you need to get the result you want. You'll soon see that loop of positivity getting stronger and stronger.

 You can get the video version of this exercise in the resources area of our website: www.sales-consultancy. com/book-resources

With your sales team

Once you have got to grips with it yourself, introduce your team to the concept of TFAR. You could use the video linked above at one of your sales meetings and share the exercise live. When I do this exercise with a group, I keep it so that they don't have to reveal the activity they're thinking about or their responses, they simply respond to the questions in their head. Give your salespeople an opportunity to share if they want to – some won't and that's fine, don't push them. You would be shining a spotlight on negative feelings and increasing their intensity, which will only make the situation worse.

Creating a no-pressure space and having rapport with your team will make it easier for people to share and be vulnerable if they want to. You'll likely find that if one person does, a couple more may follow and open discussion can flow from that. This is great for peer group learning. If nobody wants to share then that's feedback for you, suggesting that you may need a bit more practice, deeper rapport and higher levels of trust.

At the end of the session, ask your team for their new positive trigger thoughts and how they plan to put these into action. These will be much easier for them to share, but again don't push people to do so. Leave your exploration for a one-to-one conversation with them after the meeting, which you can position as check-in sessions that you're doing with everyone – a great thing to do. Focus on speaking to the more reserved or guarded salespeople first so that they get the coaching they need to start implementing this technique for themselves.

Another way of using this concept is when someone is struggling with a sales activity they need to get better at. In a one-to-one session with them, you can ask, 'What are you feeling just before you do this activity?' You'll likely uncover a negative trigger thought that needs reframing. Get them to come up with five or six alternatives – don't make any suggestions as to what these should be, they will work much better if the individual comes up with them for themselves.

Comfort Zone

The next mindset hack relates to your Comfort Zone. We all have one. It's our place of safety, where we know what we're doing and feel fully confident in our actions. But what happens when you get to the edge of your Comfort Zone?

You may stand there too scared to go over the boundary. You may feel a desire to go beyond the boundary but find other things to keep you busy, or wait for the perfect moment that never comes. You may feel so uncomfortable when you approach it that you turn round and go back to where you feel comfortable and safe.

On a more physiological level, what often happens when you get to the edge of your Comfort Zone is that your body has a response, going into fight, flight or freeze mode. This is what your body is programmed to do when it enters unchartered territory, and has been since humans first walked the earth. It's your body putting you on red alert in case something jumps out and tries to eat you. The stress response hasn't evolved since our early ancestors or it would be able to distinguish between a grizzly bear trying to eat you and trying something new at work – which definitely won't kill you.

A little anxiety about trying something new can be a good thing. When you feel it rise at the edge of your Comfort Zone, acknowledge it and thank your body for putting all your senses on full alert, ready to notice anything important while you explore this new activity. You will feel much calmer.

Most people believe that outside your Comfort Zone is a scary place, what I call the Terror Zone. In this zone, things could all go wrong, you could be humiliated, people might laugh at you, and various other scary things could happen.

It helps to know that between your Comfort Zone and the Terror Zone is a buffer, called the Learning Zone. In the Learning Zone you can try new things, make mistakes, play with, practise and perfect your new approaches. It's like the playground of the adult world.

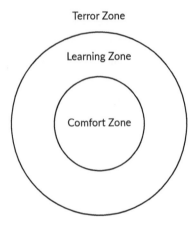

The Comfort Zone, Learning Zone and Terror Zone

If you set a goal that is too big to achieve in a few steps, you may well end up in the Terror Zone. This isn't good. It's much safer to plan your first step so that it takes you into the Learning Zone, where you can get the feedback you need, normally through mistakes – the best way of learning. This enables you to plan your next steps. You don't need to have confidence in the entire journey toward your goal, just to take the first step. This creates momentum and confidence to take the next step. . . then the next and the next.

The great news is that, as you master new skills, your Comfort Zone grows and so does your confidence. The Learning Zone never shrinks in size, so it's the perfect safeguard against the Terror Zone. Helpful, isn't it?

With your sales team

Now that you have an understanding of why people struggle to do new things, you can apply it with your salespeople.

To create a culture of personal growth, you have to allow your salespeople to make mistakes without negative repercussions. Yikes. Yes, you have to actively encourage your team to enter the Learning Zone as often as they need to without you getting annoyed if things don't go according to plan. Don't think you can pretend, either – they will feel your angry energy and decide never to enter the Learning Zone again, which would be a disaster for them and for you.

Your aim is to create a culture of psychological safety where your team feel safe to experiment, make mistakes and try again without fear of punishment. Accept that they will make mistakes on their journey to mastery. When this happens, use coaching to explore what they have learned from the experience and what they will do differently next time. Plan the next step and repeat this process again and again. Over time, what you'll end up with is a culture of proactive and courageous salespeople who go the extra mile to achieve great things. Yes, it takes time, but it's worth it.

Start by sharing this concept with your team. Actively talk about the Learning Zone in team meetings and during one-to-one sessions. Create an arena for people to share their mistakes to help others avoid them, so that you can all grow together.

The Valley of Reasons and Excuses

Imagine that you're at the bottom of a valley where the sides are really high. You can't see much of what's going on outside of it because you are right at the bottom. This is the place you go to when things are not going your way. When you're in The Valley, you come up with reasons and excuses to try and justify why you or your team are not generating the results you want.

You might think, 'I wish I had better salespeople', 'the products aren't as good as they used to be', 'our competitors are offering better deals', 'there's no budget for X, Y or Z', 'I haven't got time', 'I can't connect with the right people to make this happen' – the list of possible excuses is endless. When you do this, you relinquish all responsibility for your contribution to the shortfall in results and blame either other people or a 'something' that exists or is happening in the world outside. By blaming these external factors, you become a victim and hand over your personal power to the things you believe are the issue. It makes it even worse if any of your colleagues believe this too and you support each other in staying exactly where you are – at the bottom of The Valley, blameless and powerless.

It's uncomfortable to own your part in a failure or lack of progress. It's so much easier to blame someone or something else, isn't it? When you are blameless and powerless, though, the problem remains. Any attempt at positive action is half-hearted because deep down it's nothing to do with you – you are a victim in the situation. This reinforces your attitude of external blame and stops you taking laser-focused action.

The Valley of Reasons and Excuses...

It doesn't have to be like this. Climb out of The Valley and take a look at the landscape around you. This isn't a position from which you deny your challenges; instead, you acknowledge them fully and ask yourself:

...an alternative approach!

Asking this question allows you to regain your personal power and take positive action. You've taken back the control and the responsibility to do something about the issue.

What are the top three excuses that you use most? What negative impact do they have on your leadership?

When you admit the excuses you commonly use to make yourself feel better about a lack of results, you can start to take positive actions that move you towards getting what you want.

With your sales team

Once you can identify your own tendency to make particular excuses and attribute blame, you can start fine tuning your ears to immediately pick up on any reasons or excuses your salespeople are using to explain underperformance. Any blame language is your cue to jump in with the question: 'If this is true, what are you going to do about it?'

Initially, they may be flummoxed and not know how to answer, but persevere. Send them away to think about the problem and ask them to come back when they have a plan. When the penny drops that you'll be posing that question on a regular basis they'll start to think of the answer before you ask. Remember, repetition creates new neural pathways and behaviours.

If they are genuinely stuck, then asking the following questions in a one-to-one setting will help them to unpick the problem:

- What do you want?

- How do you want it to be?

- What do you need to get it?

- What resources do you already have that will help you get the outcome you want?

- Where are you with regards to achieving it?

- What's the next step you can take towards getting what you want?

- When will you take this step?

These questions take them out of the blame space where they are currently stuck and into a different part of the mind that focuses on creating solutions. They are great questions to have in your toolbox – you'll be surprised how often you use them with your team to help them focus on the things they can control and then do something about it.

TAKE ACTION

It's time to think about what actions you're going to take to improve your sales leadership skills and team relationships as a result of what you've read in Chapter 3. Consider what concepts resonated with you most. You could get to grips with the concept of TFAR by practising it yourself before thinking about how you can use it with your sales team or look for times when you and your team members are stepping into the Learning Zone. Identify the excuses you commonly find yourself reaching for, and the excuses you hear frequently from your team. Note these down in your journal so that you are triggered to ask the right questions when they crop up again.

4
How Beliefs Impact Wellbeing And Performance

Beliefs are assumptions that you've created at some point in your life, based on a situation you found yourself in. A belief isn't a truth or a fact; it's your perspective on something that happened to you. While beliefs feel 'real', they're not.

Take a minute to think about that. We all hold onto our beliefs and fight for them as though they were set in stone – just observe an argument between two people with opposing beliefs to see how fiercely we can cling to them.

There are two main types of belief. The first are positive, empowering beliefs. These beliefs cause you to feel great about doing a certain thing, where you know you're doing it well and you're telling yourself positive things about what's happening for you. These are the beliefs that make you feel strong and confident, ready to take on the world.

Then there are the negative, disempowering beliefs. These are the 'I can't's, the things you believe about yourself that stop you from committing to or even trying certain activities because, deep down, you believe you can't do it, or can't do it well enough.

What's particularly interesting is how these beliefs emerge. Most of them were created when you were young, in the first seven years of your life. According to sociologist Morris Massey, these are called the 'imprint years' because at this point your brain is like a sponge, taking in lots of information.[2]

During this time, you look at life through the eyes of a child without much life experience. Everything tends to be black and white, either great or terrible. You only have to observe a young child for a short time to know that they can go from big smiles, to tears, and back to big smiles in a fraction of a second. To them, things are always either good or bad. In these formative years, the things that happen to you cause you to form beliefs that you will often carry with you for the rest of your life. Some of these are positive, others less so.

---

2   'Values Development', Changing Minds, no date, http://changingminds.org/explanations/values/values_development.htm

Let's consider an example. Imagine a child observing the adults around them drinking from a bottle of water. They decide they want to do it too. (That's how children learn.) So they pick up the bottle of water and try to get the top off. An adult sees them and says, 'Oh, no. Don't do it like that, that's wrong. Give me the bottle and I'll open it for you.' They open the bottle and give it to the child.

The next time the child wants to open the bottle of water, they'll have another go. They might turn the bottle the other way around. The adult sees them and they say, 'No, no, don't do that, you'll get water all over the floor. Give it to me, I'll open it for you.'

How many times do you think this needs to happen before the child looks at that bottle of water and decides to pass it to an adult to open because they think they can't open it themselves? Around six times on average.

The child might then decide that they can't do other things. 'I can't draw as well as Suzy', 'I can't ride my bike as well as Johnny', 'I can't pass exams as well as Peter. I can't do X as well as that person. I can't, I can't, I can't.' These beliefs all stack up on one another, and even when they are able to open a bottle of water, to draw a picture and to ride a bicycle, even when they have proven to themselves that they can do all those things, the belief that 'I can't' stays with them. This is why when we get to the edge of our Comfort Zone and try to do something new, we can be pulled back into that 'I can't' belief, even though it's not true.

If you're not achieving the success you want as a sales leader, it's quite likely that negative beliefs are holding you back. You may be conscious of some of them, but you need to identify those that are unconscious too.

The great news is that you can change these negative beliefs. You will have already done this before. When you were a small child, perhaps you believed in Father Christmas or the Tooth Fairy. Do you still believe in them today? There will be lots of other things you believed as a child that you no longer believe. . . this is evidence that you are already capable of changing your beliefs.

It's also worth pointing out that all the negative beliefs that affect your sales leadership will also be affecting other areas of your life. Look for patterns and start to become more aware of what your limiting beliefs are. Take notice of the language you use – 'I can't' is your red flag.

Your 'I can't' list

To apply your new understanding of negative and limiting beliefs, we're going to try a quick exercise.

EXERCISE: 'I can't' list

In your journal write a list of all the sales leadership activities you feel apprehensive about, the ones you avoid, the ones that trigger negative feelings or thoughts. The sales leadership activities that immediately spark an 'I can't' response.

A quick reality check here: there are hundreds of 'I can't' thoughts spinning around our minds, all the time. You are not alone. We all have them lurking in the background. You don't need to share this list with anyone, so be totally honest with yourself. The more you uncover, the more you will get from completing this exercise.

Keep writing until your mind goes blank. This is your first blank spot.

Repeat the thought. 'I can't' over and over – this gives your mind an instruction to dig a bit deeper. Do this until your thoughts start to flow again and you can add more 'I can't's to your list. Eventually, you will reach another blank spot. Again, repeat the thought 'I can't' until you can go beyond this second blank spot. Pushing beyond at least two blank spots will give your list greater depth.

The important thing is to uncover as many of these beliefs as you can – the more you uncover, the more you can get rid of. Remember, you don't need to share these with anyone. Carry the list around with you for a few days and add any 'I can't' statements that you notice yourself saying or thinking.

Creating this list will grow your self-awareness. When you know what's going on in your belief system, you get the opportunity to get rid of limiting beliefs forever and replace them with positive and empowering ones.

Busting your 'I can't's

Now you have your list of I can't statements, it's time
to learn how to replace these thoughts with something
positive and empowering, which we'll do through a
series of exercises. This process should take around
thirty minutes initially, but it's super powerful and gets
quicker every time you do it. You'll need to understand
the full process so that you know how to help your
salespeople shift their own negative beliefs.

First things first, you need to find yourself a quiet place
where you won't be disturbed. Turn off your phone and
remove any distractions that might get in the way. Once
you have found a corner of peace and quiet, we can get
started.

Return to your 'I can't' list. Pick the belief that has the
biggest negative impact on your sales leadership and
your sales team. Write it down on a sheet of paper or a
post-it and put it where you can see it.

I'm going to walk you through a journey that needs your
focus, honesty and openness. You'll be travelling through
the following phases:

- Phase 1: Discovering your inner landscape

- Phase 2: Destabilising the foundations of your 'I
  can't'

- Phase 3: Reframing and defining your 'I can'

- Phase 4: Reinforcing your 'I can'

Each phase will have questions for you to answer – either in your head, out loud or in your journal. You can work through all of the phases one after the other, or take a break between each. Do what works for you.

Ready? Let's get started. . .

PHASE 1: Discovering your inner landscape

I want you to imagine yourself twelve months from now. You're still holding onto your 'I can't' thought. Nothing has changed.

What price will you have paid for holding onto this negative thought?

What will have been the impact on you, and on your sales team?

Take your time and think it through. This may not be easy if you've never thought about it in this way before. Give your imagination permission to play out the consequences in full technicolour.

Feeling uncomfortable?

It's OK to feel that way right now. In fact, the more uncomfortable this feels, the better your result will be.

Now think about five years into the future.

If you change nothing at all, what price will you pay then?

Where will you be as a sales leader?

How about your sales team?

Will you still have a job?

Again, take your time and think it through. You may not be feeling your best right now – that's OK. Stick with me.

Now scrub those images away and let's move onto something positive. Think about your life without that nasty 'I can't' belief.

How will changing this belief improve your sales leadership and your life? Take your time to think about all the good stuff that would happen.

What would you be able to do more of?

Who would you be as a person?

These are the potential consequences for your future. Tap into and really engage with these positive feelings – feels good, doesn't it?

Let's explore the impact of your negative thought on your past.

How has this negative thought blocked you?

What has it stopped you from doing or achieving?

Think about all the times you've hesitated or avoided these actions that you knew would help you be more successful. Also consider the things you've avoided outside of work.

Now that you've reflected on what this thought has stopped you from doing, what will you lose if you don't let go of your negative belief?

Take all the time you need to think about this. Let your mind go wherever it wants to so that you get the insights you need.

Now check in with yourself – how committed are you to letting go of your negative belief?

Anything less than 100% will limit the results of this exercise. If you are totally committed to letting go of this negative belief then you can move onto the next phase. Resistance generally occurs because of fear. If you're not quite there with this belief, pick something easier for now to build your confidence. You can always revisit any particularly challenging negative beliefs later on.

Once you have identified a negative belief that you are fully committed to overcoming, you are ready to move on to the next phase. Take all the time you need to reflect and respond to the questions asked in these phases – there's no rushing this process. Take a break if you need to process or rest.

PHASE 2: Destabilising the foundations of your 'I can't'

Look again at the 'I can't' belief you have chosen to remove. Why do you believe this negative thought about yourself? Uncover as many reasons as you can.

When did you take on this negative thought? You may not know consciously. . . so if you were to think of a number, what's the first number that pops into your head?

That's possibly how old you were when this negative thought was created by you.

And if you don't remember. . . that really doesn't matter.

When we repeatedly do something, it means that it is positively serving us in some way. How has this negative belief served you in a positive way in the past?

The answer may not come immediately, but a common one is that when people believe 'I can't do X', it stops them from doing it. Because they never do it, they never fail at it.

Might your negative belief be helping you feel better about yourself in some way? Could it be protecting you? Where has it been useful? Take all the time you need to reflect what your reasons are for believing this thought about yourself.

Now think of an example of when, in the past, you've exhibited the behaviour that your negative belief says you can't do. This may take some thought, so take all the time you need. Explore other areas of your life where you have done the opposite of your negative thought, beyond sales leadership or work. This helps you dig a little deeper. For example, when a client tells me they can't confidently deliver challenging feedback, they can often recount experiences outside of work where they find it easy to do just that. Take all the time you need to come up with an example of when you have shown that you *can* do the very thing that your 'I can't' belief is stopping you from doing. This is an important part of the process.

Once you have got your example, take yourself back to that situation and relive it from start to finish.

- What are you doing?
- What are you seeing?
- What are you hearing?
- What are you feeling?
- What are you thinking?

Go through it slowly, noticing as much detail as possible and bringing to mind the thoughts and feelings you experienced at the time; tap into the positive energy. Now how are you feeling?

Note how it's more challenging to remember the good stuff. This is because your mind more easily pulls out memories that are aligned with your thinking, so if you have a negative thought, associated negative memories will surface more easily. Any positive memories get left in the archives. Unless you ask your mind to open that file, they will remain hidden away.

Now that you understand that there are loads of counter examples of your negative belief in the archives of your mind, I want you to find another one. When you have thought of one – remember, it needs to be a specific event – then repeat the exercise. Take yourself back to the situation and relive this second event from start to finish, following the exact same process described above.

Really associate into the event.

- What are you doing?
- What are you seeing?
- What are you hearing?
- What are you feeling?
- What are you thinking?

Take your time to go through the event slowly. . . noticing as much detail as possible and bringing to mind the thoughts and feelings you were experiencing at the time. How are you feeling after reliving this second positive example? Your mind will likely be getting better at this now it's got into the swing of things, so let's look for a third example. Remember that you can choose situations from any area of your life, and they need to be specific. Again, take yourself back and relive the experience from start to finish. Really associate into the event.

- What are you doing?
- What are you seeing?
- What are you hearing?
- What are you feeling?
- What are you thinking?

Take your time to go through the event slowly. . . noticing as much detail as possible and bringing to mind the thoughts and feelings you were experiencing at the time. Remember to tap into the positive energy of your positive actions.

Well done you. Congratulations on finding three examples of positive behaviour that disproves your negative, limiting belief about yourself. How are you feeling at the end of this experience? Acknowledge your achievement and congratulate yourself – you should be feeling pretty good.

Now that we've removed your 'I can't', it's time to replace it with something new.

PHASE 3: Reframing and defining your 'I can'

Having relived three positive examples that contradict your negative thought, what do you believe now? How do you feel about yourself now that your thinking has changed? Drawing on your past experiences, create a positive belief that taps into and captures your positive behaviour.

Whatever your 'I can't' was, what does overcoming it mean you *can* do now?

Make sure that your empowering belief is stated in positive terms, emphasising the behaviour that you want rather than the one you don't. For example, 'I don't get stressed' is not a positive belief, but 'I can stay calm when I'm under stress' is.

Take all the time you need to come up with a positive belief that resonates with you and that feels good when you say it. Once you have it, write down your new empowering belief in your journal.

Now that you've completed the first three phases, it's time to click your new, positive 'I can' belief into place.

PHASE 4: Reinforcing your 'I can'

The next step is to visualise yourself embracing this new positive thought. Really take it in and embody it. What does that feel like?

Notice all the ways in which you feel more positive, more confident, happier. Notice all the positive emotions that are coming up for you.

Now I want you to step into the future and imagine a situation where the old 'I can't' thought would have surfaced. What is different now that your belief has changed?

Take your time visualising your new behaviour from start to finish, noticing as much detail as possible:

- What are you doing differently?
- What are you seeing?
- What are you hearing?
- What are you feeling?
- What are you thinking?

This should feel good – relish your accomplishment.

Now let's find another one. Think of another situation, maybe in a different context, and again, visualise your new behaviour from start to finish, noticing as much detail as possible guided by the questions:

- What are you doing differently?
- What are you seeing?
- What are you hearing?
- What are you feeling?
- What are you thinking?

Be sure to enjoy all the positive emotions that come up. Your mind will be getting into the swing of it now and will know what you want it to do going forward.

You are rewiring your thinking, so let's lock it in by tapping into the power of three with one more imagined future situation.

Again, take your time to imagine, in detail, how you will behave differently and how that feels. What are you doing now?

- What are you doing differently?
- What are you seeing?
- What are you hearing?

- What are you feeling?
- What are you thinking?

Enjoy the new you! How do you feel about that old negative thought now?

Can you even remember what it was?

Congratulations – you've just got rid of your first negative 'I can't' belief and created the first of many empowering 'I can' beliefs. You can begin to enjoy the new you.

In order to fully embed your new positive belief, you must train your unconscious mind. The more you repeat it to yourself in the first six to ten days, the quicker your mind will incorporate your new behaviour going forward. You can write notes and put them in places that you look at often. You can have it as a reminder or alarm on your phone. You can record it and play it to yourself frequently during the day. You can recite it in your bathroom mirror. Do what works for you. I find the best times are first thing in the morning and last thing at night. The more often you recite your new positive belief, the quicker you will embed it.

You now have a process you can use over and over again to shrink your list of 'I can't's and create a new list of 'I can's.

With your sales team

Now that you know how to get rid of your own negative beliefs, you'll be much better equipped to help your sales team remove and replace theirs. The first step is to notice where they have them. It will be in the areas they are either struggling with or avoiding.

Ask them how they feel before doing such an activity. Listen to their language. If they say they can't do something because of X, Y or Z you can get their negative belief out into the open. You don't have to go through the whole repeated process I shared with you, simply asking the questions will start to destabilise those negative thoughts.

Providing positive counter examples is an excellent way to create doubt about their 'I can't' belief. For example, if one of your team says 'I can't deliver presentations', but you've seen them display the relevant behaviours and skills in a non-presentation situation, such as telling a story to a captivated group of people, share this with them. The first time you do this they may respond with something like, 'That was a fluke.' The second time you do it, they may consider it more seriously. The third time, they will start to believe you. You can follow up by asking, 'What do you believe now?'

If a salesperson has a deep-rooted negative belief, you may have to go through the entire process of challenging and replacing this belief with them in a one-to-one session. Or give them the audio version of the exercise to do on their own and discuss it afterwards. You'll find a link to the audio version at the end of this chapter. Trust your gut feeling on what is right for that person based on what you know about them.

The more negative beliefs you help your salespeople change, the more confident, motivated and successful your team will become. Before we move on, it's important for you to understand that your beliefs, both positive and negative, could have a detrimental impact on your team. If you have been a successful salesperson and you believe certain aspects of sales to be easy, you may project that onto others. This could drain their confidence in their ability to master the skill in their own way. Be careful not to belittle any of your team's negative beliefs by imposing your positive one. We are all in different places of our life journey and it is wise to remember that, especially in the context of beliefs.

TAKE ACTION

Think about what actions you're going to take as a result of the exercise you've completed in this chapter.

You may choose to eliminate additional negative beliefs of your own before using this approach with your team, or you may choose to help a member of your team who's finding it particularly hard to get past their negative thoughts.

Focus on the actions that will create the biggest positive impact on your own and your team's mindset and behavioural change will quickly follow.

If you would like a guided audio version of the exercise, to use yourself or with your team, you can download the audio here: www.sales-consultancy.com/book-resources

---

5

Creating A Healthy Sales Growth Mindset Culture

According to Carol Dweck, a psychologist and Professor at Stanford University, there are two types of mindset: a Fixed Mindset and a Growth Mindset, which she defines as follows:[3]

> 'In a **Fixed Mindset**, people believe their basic qualities, like their intelligence or talent, are simply fixed traits. . . .
>
> In a **Growth Mindset**, people believe that their most basic abilities can be developed through dedication and hard work – brains and talent are just the starting point.'

---

3   C Dweck, *Mindset: Changing the way you think to fulfil your potential* (Robinson, 2017)

You will have a blend of mindsets in your team; some will be fully Growth Mindset, some will have a fully Fixed Mindset, and for others their mindset will vary depending on the situation. Your salespeople that naturally have a Growth Mindset are more likely to be your high performers, the ambitious ones who want more and develop themselves to be more. The only way to develop a team of salespeople with a Growth Mindset that continually strive for greater success is to be a Sales Growth Mindset Leader.

What is a Sales Growth Mindset Leader?

In a nutshell, this is a sales leader who creates an environment where salespeople feel comfortable to step outside their Comfort Zone, try new things and learn from their mistakes, without fear of negative consequences. To determine whether you are currently this kind of sales leader, ponder on the following questions:

- Do you tell your salespeople the best way to get results, according to you?

- Have you ever got mad when someone in your team has done something that hasn't worked out?

- Have you ever raised your voice or expressed your frustration with your team?

- Do your sales team play it safe?

- Do they tell you what they think you want to hear?

- Are your team reactive rather than proactive?

- Do your sales team agree to do something then not deliver?

Your responses may be different for each salesperson, but taking a straw poll, if you mostly responded 'yes' then you are probably not a Sales Growth Mindset Leader.

You will want to do something about this, because the benefits of creating a Sales Growth Mindset Culture are tangible. When I work with sales teams to create this kind of environment, we tend to see a sales increases of at least 20% across the team. Some salespeople even double their sales, simply because they are thinking differently and the sales leadership approach has changed to support their growth. This isn't a 'nice to have', it's an essential element of sales and leadership success. So if you're not already there, what can you start doing now to create this in your team?

It starts with you. You are the foundations upon which everything else sits. You are the catalyst for change. It won't be a quick win, it's a long game with massive rewards but there will be lots of wins along the way and things will keep getting better and better.

The seven Sales Growth Mindset Leadership traits

There are seven leadership traits that are crucial when creating a Sales Growth Mindset Culture. Your mission, if you choose to accept it, is to master these traits. Some of them you will already have, some you may not be great at and some are nowhere to be seen. That's fine – none of us is perfect, but we should all be striving to be the best version of ourselves. Here are the seven traits that you can develop in your leadership.

1. Open-minded and curious

- Explore all opportunities and be curious about what's below the surface, for your sales team and your clients.

- Keep up with the latest thinking on mindset leadership and continually integrate strategies that improve mindset development and boost sales results.

- Be open to new ideas, including those from your sales team.

- Continuously look to improve yourself and your sales team.

2. Comfortable with being uncomfortable

- Embrace uncertainty and unpick ambiguity to find previously unseen opportunities.

- It's imperative that you get buy-in from your sales team to ensure they don't fear uncertainty and instead embrace it, to create momentum and build their confidence.

- Identify what's within your Comfort Zone and what's outside it – and have a plan to go into your Learning Zone as much as possible.

3. Strong situational awareness

- Focus on exploring the deeper reading of a situation – see around, beneath and beyond what is immediately obvious.

- Check yourself. Sales leaders often don't have a Growth Mindset because their experience and certainty get in the way of exploring new possibilities.

- Take your expanded understanding and project what is required in the future to achieve your desired outcomes.

4. Ownership and accountability

- Take responsibility for your own and your team's performance. What could you do differently to increase results?

- A Sales Growth Mindset demands resilience and delivers value. What could you do to increase this?

- Seek to eliminate complacency and mediocrity in yourself and your team.

- Identify your contribution to poor results and what you could do differently going forward.

- Be clear on what is expected from you as a leader – know what results you are expected to deliver so that you can focus on the required actions.

5. Growth

- The days of salespeople thinking their leader has all the answers are gone – Sales Growth Mindset Leaders grow *with* their team.

- Create environments of greater intimacy in which you and your sales team can grow and evolve together.

- You all have strengths and weaknesses, acknowledge them and strive to improve.

- Sales Growth Mindset Leaders let go of their egos – you are not the star of the show.

6. Collaboration

- Work as a team, for the good of the team.

- Develop strong relationships, communication and understanding with other departments that impact on sales.

- Seek alignment to identify, create or strengthen opportunities.

- Be more inclusive to create an entrepreneurial attitude to sales growth.

- Create, build and maintain relationships across the organisation.

7. A focus on people

- Remember that it's not about you, it's about your ability to inspire your sales team beyond where they currently are.

- Build trust, confidence and the ability to navigate the needs of your salespeople.

- Continuously nudge your salespeople into their Learning Zone and support them towards growth and greater success.

- Coach, give feedback and have those difficult conversations – this is vital for a Sales Growth Mindset Culture.

- Create a culture that your salespeople truly believe in and can align with.

- Focus on creating growth that will take your salespeople and the organisation to higher levels of success.

- Develop a clear understanding of the individuals in your sales team and their specific needs.

The world is constantly evolving and we are currently transitioning from a knowledge-based economy to a wisdom-based economy. It's no longer about what you know, it's about what you do with what you know.

Over the years I've worked with sales leaders that have ranged from doing absolutely none of these things, to lots. What is common to all sales leaders, in my experience, is that they are always able to cultivate these traits easily once they know what they are and how to start enacting them. It takes discipline and determination to change existing habits but the rewards are more than worth it.

Growth Mindset research

When Carol Dweck did her seminal study of Growth Mindset in children twenty years ago, she found that how you praise someone can lead to a dramatic shift in their behaviours:[4]

- Of children who had been praised for their intelligence, 86% asked for information about how their peers did on the same task.

- Only 23% of children who had been praised for effort asked how they compared to others; the majority asked for feedback on how they could improve.

- Students who had been praised for their natural ability were more likely to choose easier tasks going forward, lie about how successful they had been, they enjoyed the tasks less and were more likely to give up quickly.

As a result of her findings, Dweck cautioned against too much praise of effort:

'We need to remember that effort is a means to an end. The goal is learning and improving.'[5]

The focus of Growth Mindset is learning, not simply trying hard. This means you need to focus on nudging your team into their Learning Zone through manageable steps with an emphasis on learning, developing and getting results. When one of your team uses Fixed

---

4   CM Mueller and CS Dweck, 'Praise for intelligence can undermine children's motivation and performance', *J Pers Soc Psychol*, 1998, 75(1): 33–52, https://pubmed.ncbi.nlm.nih.gov/9686450/
5   C Dweck, 'Carol Dweck revisits the Growth Mindset', Prism, no date, http://prism.scholarslab.org/prisms/66cb28fe-7d8d-11e5-9ea7-3ef7d8f21ed1/visualize?locale=es

Mindset language, you can follow it with something reassuring and more in line with a Growth Mindset. Over time, they will start thinking in this way for themselves. I've provided some examples below of how you can use language to move someone from a Fixed to a Growth Mindset.

Developing a Growth Mindset

Statement...	Respond with...
I'm no good at this.	What do you need to get better at this?
I'll never be good enough.	With time and effort you will get better.
I give up.	What can you do instead?
Things haven't gone to plan.	Let's go for Plan B.
I got it wrong.	Mistakes are part of developing yourself.
This is too hard.	This is going to take time and practice.
It's good enough.	Are you really showing up as your best self?
I'm not getting this as well as others.	You can learn from them.

TAKE ACTION

It's time to think about what actions you're going to take to create a Sales Growth Mindset Culture.

Be sure to focus on actions that improve your sales leadership skills for the benefit of your team, helping you to become a Sales Growth Mindset Leader and develop a Sales Growth Mindset Culture – a psychologically safe culture that supports growth, evolution and success.

Use the seven leadership traits as a guide – start with the traits that are a quick win for you. This will help build your confidence to tackle the more challenging ones.

6

Understanding Your People

The route to understanding is conversation. Psychometric tests will only give you knowledge of your salespeople's traits, not of the human beings behind the traits. Their life stories. Their pains and tragedies. Their joys and happy events. Their sense of humour. Their values and how they interpret them. How they treat others. How much they smile. Their complexities. How warm they are. And everything else that makes each human being a beautiful, unique creation.

To understand your people, the first step is to understand their map of the world – this is how they view the world, how they navigate it and how they like to travel. Let's dive in.

Navigating your salespeople's map of the world

We each have a unique way of perceiving the world; this is our map of the world. Your map has been created by all the experiences you've had, from the moment you were born to the present day. It's the same for all of us. The family you grew up with, your teachers, your friends, your holidays, the people who have influenced you along the way, all the films you've watched, the books you've read – everything you have experienced has gone into creating the person you are today.

Thinking about this, let me ask you: how likely is it that another person could have had the exact same life experiences and reacted to them in the exact same way as you? The answer is it's impossible. If you have siblings, you'll know that even in the same family environment everyone has distinct personalities, characteristics and preferences.

Your map of the world is as unique as your DNA, and when you're out there communicating with your team in an effort to influence and motivate them, you'll do so in a way that is based on your map of the world. All your communication is a reflection of what's going on inside you. If you're excited, you'll communicate your message with an excited energy, regardless of whether it's the most digestible way for your message to land with the other person.

Understanding others' maps

It's crucial to understand what really going on in your salesperson's map. What thoughts and feelings do they have around specific sales activities they are avoiding? How confident are they in their abilities? What do they think about the company and culture? What issues are they having? What do they need help with? What do they want in their career and life? Where are their mindset gaps?

The surest way of developing a high-performing salesperson is to understand their map of the world – the landscape, the valleys, the mountains and the view they are focusing on. And the only way you can do this is to put your map of the world aside and uncover their map by asking 'you'-focused coaching questions. When you ask these questions in an environment of trust and good rapport, your salesperson will find it much easier to open up with honesty and vulnerability. Holding a space for them to do this is crucial. This means asking questions, then listening – not always easy when you're a sales leader who likes to fix things. Remember that every time you jump in to fix something for someone you are stalling their development. You are imposing your own map and making them feel small.

Excessive telling

Sales leaders can sometimes fall into the trap of talking about themselves and how they did things when they were a salesperson. It's natural to want to share what worked for you in order to help your team, but it doesn't work long term.

When you start sharing what you would do in a situation, not only are you in danger of switching your salesperson off, which you don't want to do as this stops them listening... you are also unconsciously telling them that they are not good enough to make decisions for themselves. You're also sending the message that you're not interested in how they would do it. This leads to passive compliance and a lack of proactivity in your team. Why would they be innovative, proactive and try new things when you have all the answers and already know how you'd like them to do things? They will never be as motivated to succeed with your plan of action as they will be with their own. They will have a vested interest in their plan succeeding. If your plan fails, you can't blame them. It was your plan; they are in the clear. That's how they will rationalise it. Don't make them feel irrelevant. Make them the star of the show. Support them in creating and implementing their own plan.

It's so important to understand what's going on below the surface with each of your team. Imagine that each salesperson is a jigsaw puzzle. You only have a few pieces so you can't make out the bigger picture they are part of. Every time you ask a question that uncovers something below the surface, you get another piece of the puzzle. You'll need a lot of puzzle pieces before you can start to make out the overall picture. Until you know what that picture – their map of the world – looks like, you have no real sense of what actions or approaches you could take to positively impact that salesperson.

If what you are doing isn't working with certain salespeople, it's likely you haven't got full clarity or understanding of their map of the world. Instead of telling, judging or assuming, start being interested in and curious about each salesperson and commit to finding out as much as you can about them.

Here are some questions to get you started:

- What inspires you to get up in the morning?

- What would you like to achieve in the next twelve months?

- What will that give you?

- What activities would you like to be better at?

- What do you think your barriers are?

- What stops you?

- What would you like instead?

- What else?

- What would happen if you did?

- What would happen if you didn't?

- What wouldn't happen if you did?

- What wouldn't happen if you didn't? (You might get a blank look with this one but stay silent and wait for their answer, it's likely to be insightful for you and for them.)

All these questions focus on the salesperson; they are the only one who can answer them. When you ask 'you'-focused questions, you open up the conversation. Your questions show that you're interested and you care. Their answers will provide you more pieces of the puzzle, giving you the clues and insights you need to support each salesperson with what they need in order to be awesome. Your actions can then be guided by their map, their territory and their psychology.

If you sense any resistance from your salesperson in a conversation, it's a sign of a lack of rapport – you may be going too fast. Slow down, build rapport and go at their pace.

I know I've told you to be quiet and listen – and it's important to do that – but there are some occasions where you can share what other salespeople have done in a similar situation. Do not suggest they do the same, simply offer it as an option. Highlight colleagues with a similar personality who they may relate to. If you focus on your top performer, you may inadvertently make them feel inadequate. Remember: don't compare one salesperson's chapter five to another's chapter twenty-five.

Rapport is crucial for your exploration. Remember to ask, listen and respond – ideally with another question. Watch their journey unfold and let them determine the route and pace. In my experience, you're likely to learn useful stuff for yourself along the way. Creating a culture like this reinforces trust, openness and honesty, which is incredibly powerful and leads to big strides in personal growth and sales success. You are creating psychological safety for your salespeople to grow in the best way for them.

It's important to state here that you don't have to agree with anyone's map of the world, you simply have to acknowledge it as their truth and have it as your starting point in any developmental conversation. If you try and drag them into your map they will resist, so go where they are and lead them gently in the direction they need to travel.

This also applies to your written communications, like emails or texts.

Spend as much time in their map as you can to build your relationship and increase their motivation to grow, to be more and to succeed.

Preferences

We all have preferences that influence our patterns of behaviour and thought. These preferences adapt and change depending on the situation we are in. Over twenty years ago, I discovered Meta Programmes, the patterns that influence everything we do. Since then, I've noticed them every single day in myself and in others.

Knowing what your preferences are in any given context allows you to either leverage them if appropriate, or develop counter strategies so that you can show up as your best leader self. Being able to also identify the preferences of your salespeople enables you to better understand their map of the world and to tailor your communication so that it is more likely to land in the way that you intend.

In my experience, friction is most prevalent when opposing Meta Programmes are at play. Think of preferences as a continuum; you can sit at either end or anywhere along the continuum. Imagine a coin in the middle of that continuum. This is the context or situation and you can view it from either side of the coin. For example, do you view underperforming salespeople as a nuisance in your life, ruining your opportunities, limiting your success and status? Or do you view them as an opportunity to grow your leadership skills, a natural part of leading a sales team, people who need your support to show up as their best selves? Both perspectives are valid – the situation isn't right or wrong, good or bad, it just is. It is your Meta Programme that determine the story you tell yourself.

Meta Programmes

Much of the initial work on Meta Programmes was undertaken by Leslie Cameron-Bandler[6] in the USA and it was one of her students, Rodger Bailey, who first adapted and used her work in the business context.[7] Bailey also developed a series of questions that uncover a person's Meta Programmes, to create the Language and Behaviour (LAB) Profile. This method has been popularised over recent years by Shelle Rose Charvet, author of *Words That Change Minds*.[8]

Different theorists identify different Meta Programmes. For example, in *Figuring Out People*,[9] Bodenhammer and Hall identify fifty-one Meta Programmes, whereas O'Connor and Seymour, in *Introducing Neuro-Linguistic*

6   'Meta Programmes', Institute of Applied Psychology, no date, https://iap.edu. au/meta-programmes
7   KE Rice, 'Meta-programmes', 2016, KE Rice Integrated SocioPsychology Pages, www.integratedsociopsychology.net/theory/meta-programmes
8   SR Charvet, *Words That Change Minds: The 14 patterns for mastering the language of influence*, third edition (Bloomanity LLC, 2019)
9   ML Hall and BG Bodenhamer, *Figuring Out People: Reading people using meta-programs* (Neuro Semantic Publications, 1997)

Programming,[10] identify only seven. In some cases, different labels are given to the same or similar programmes – for example, Match/Mismatch equates to Sameness/ Difference. I'm going to give you my take on what I believe to be the most important Meta Programmes in sales and sales leadership.

Your Meta Programmes are established in childhood and are highly likely to remain set unless a significant emotional event rewires your thinking – something like the death of a loved one, a serious illness, a relationship break-up, something life-changing.

Context dependent

It's important to remember that Meta Programmes are context dependent and may change in different situations. For example, the way you behave in a personal relationship may be different to the way you act with the people in your team. This means you should be on the lookout for when significant things are happening in a salesperson's personal life. When a salesperson's behaviour changes out of the blue that's a red flag for you to investigate what's going on for them in a one-to-one session. Behaviours rarely change without a significant trigger and may indicate that the person needs additional support.

_____

10   J O'Connor and J Seymour, *Introducing Neuro-Linguistic Programming* (Aquarian Press, 1990)

Keep in mind. . .

Our preferences are already in place by the time we are seven years old but it's important to remember that they are context/situation-dependent.

It's also important to remember that a person is not exclusively a one preference type of person, the situation or context will determine which preference shows up. We all display different preferences in different aspects of our lives. This is great because it means we can more easily switch when we identify a difference between our preference and the preferences of the people around us. Just because you don't usually have one preference in a particular context, doesn't mean you can't. It just takes a bit of practice. Once you have identified how each of your salespeople's preferences play out in different contexts, you have a blueprint for how to masterfully lead them in any situation. This is best for their growth and development, and makes it much easier for you to show up as your best self.

You'll notice that you get on better and more easily with the salespeople who have the same preference as you, this is only human. We like people who are like us. This isn't helpful when you lead a team of salespeople with a range of preferences. You will have all types of people in your team (unless you have recruited in your likeness, which is common). Having a team who all share the same preferences leads to an imbalance and weakness – you'll all agree with each other and be limited in what you notice, do and achieve.

You are leading a sales team with differing preferences, which means you are the one who has to adapt if you're to support their development, growth and sales success. This requires an ability to analyse what you see, hear and feel when observing your team. Tailoring your leadership to suit different preferences will support your salespeople in a truly positive way and allow them to flourish, grow and show up as their best selves. This is definitely a skill worth mastering, as Meta Programmes impact so strongly on motivation. When you master the ability to interpret what you observe, you will have found the key that unlocks the door to each salesperson's success. Be particularly mindful of your team members' Meta Programme preferences whenever you're nudging them out of their Comfort Zone into their Learning Zone. You'll face much less resistance and more motivation to move forward.

Keeping all of the above in mind, let's dive into the first Meta Programme.

Towards/Away From

At a broad level, there are two essential motivations: pain and pleasure. You are constantly seeking to minimise one or maximise the other. Think of an outcome you want in either the short or the long term, what makes this outcome so attractive to you? What will getting this outcome do for you? Will it give you pleasure, or will it move you Away From pain and discomfort?

Ask one of your salespeople what their desired outcomes are and the reasons they are important to them. Some people will talk about being unhappy or uncomfortable in their current situation, suggesting an 'Away From' motivation, while others will share how getting this outcome will have a positive impact on their lives, indicating a 'Towards' motivation. Ask a person how they came to buy their current car. Was it because of their dissatisfaction with their old car (Away From), or was it because they particularly liked and enjoyed driving their new one (Towards)?

It would be a mistake to think that a 'Towards' preference is positive and therefore always good and an 'Away From' preference is negative and always bad. Imagine being in a burning building – an Away From strategy would be helpful here. Like all other Meta Programmes, Towards and Away From are just different ends of the continuum, different ways of being, and not in themselves good or bad. Depending upon circumstances, one strategy or orientation might be more useful or appropriate than another.

When setting goals, it is far more useful to move Towards what you want rather than Away From what you don't want. You get what you focus on, so your chances of success are increased when you have clarity about what it is you're striving for. If you want to give something up, knowing your Towards/Away From preference can enhance your ability to increase your willpower. For example, if you tend to move Towards, think of the benefits you'll get when you have given up. If you have an Away From preference, you should focus on the consequences of not giving up.

In the context of sales leadership, you will likely be familiar with the carrot and stick principle. A sales incentive is a carrot – but carrots will only inspire salespeople with a Towards preference. Your salespeople with an Away From preference are likely to focus on why they are unlikely to achieve the carrot. They are more driven by the fear of a negative experience and therefore will respond more positively to a little stick prodding. Language like, 'You don't want to miss out, do you?' will motivate them to move away from the pain of non-achievement.

The most noticeable traits of someone with a Towards preference include:

- Self-motivated

- Driven

- Goal-focused

- Uses language like 'want', 'attain', 'achieve', 'gain', 'get', 'obtain' and 'secure'

- Can be blinkered, especially at times of great focus

- Often leaves a trail of destruction behind them (they rarely look back) in the pursuit of their goals

- Can be overly positive and not see issues coming until it's too late

The most noticeable traits of someone with an Away From preference include:

- Great problem solver

- Notices potential issues way ahead of others

- Strong desire not to fail

- Uses language like 'don't want', 'avoid', 'dodge', 'exclude', 'get rid of' and 'side-step'

- Pain averse so less likely to try new things

- Low risk appetite

- Often perceived as negative because they focus on what could go wrong

Influencing strategy

To motivate a salesperson that has a Towards preference, establish and emphasise their desired goals and outcomes. Share how moving forward will help them get what they want and focus on the benefits they will receive. It's no surprise that people with a Towards preference are often attracted to a career in sales.

To motivate a salesperson with an Away From preference, establish what they don't want and reinforce the uncomfortable consequences of not taking action to prevent this. Emphasise that you can help them to avoid what they don't want. Identify any potential problems and reassure them that these can be decreased or eliminated when they take the required action. You may also need to address any mindset barriers to taking action. The TFAR approach in Chapter 3 would help in this situation.

Remember that preferences can change in different contexts. You may notice in your Towards-oriented salespeople that, when things are not going well, they could adopt an Away From strategy – as could you. This is because the situation has changed, creating more uncertainty and fear, for example at times of economic or industry challenge.

Internal/External

How do you know that you've done a good job? If you have an External point of reference, you will know because someone has given you feedback or you achieve a set goal. On the other hand, if you have an Internal orientation, you'll just know.

Some salespeople are eager to please while others are so wrapped up in what they're doing, they just get on with things. An External preference salesperson is influenced by what other people think and say; positive feedback makes them feel good and negative feedback makes them feel bad.

We've mentioned the carrot and the stick as ways to motivate people. Some sales leaders think these are the only two ways to motivate people. However, both these methods of communication and motivation only work with your Externally referenced salespeople.

The Internally referenced salesperson doesn't require any feedback to validate them. They have an inner calibration that tells them the criteria they need to meet to do a good job. If they are not told what specifically is required, they will make up their own minds about what constitutes good performance. The result will then be totally dependent on their criteria and standards. If their inner criteria and standards are low, they will assume they have done a good job even if they haven't. The opposite is also true; if their criteria and standards are super high, they will think they've done a poor job when in fact they have done a brilliant job. Internally oriented people need a reality check sometimes.

If you are an Internally referenced sales leader, you need to be more mindful of giving feedback – you don't personally need it, so you may be unlikely to give it naturally. You may also be more likely to dismiss other people's opinions if they are not aligned with your own. If you are Externally referenced, you are more likely to be swayed by what others say so should keep this in mind.

The most noticeable traits of someone with an Internal orientation include:

- Can often be perceived as not listening

- Has their own inner criteria for success

- Is not swayed by feedback when it's not aligned with their inner criteria

- Is uncomfortable with positive feedback – say it once and move on

- Has an inner sense that they are right, which can be frustrating when they are not

The most noticeable traits of someone with an External orientation include:

- Needs feedback or external data to be certain they have done a good job

- Is more likely to check that they are doing things correctly in the learning stages

- Is easier to influence with data and feedback

- Needs positive encouragement to be at their best

- Is more likely to be wounded by constructive/ developmental feedback

Influencing strategy

To influence an Internally referenced salesperson, ask them questions that enable them to internalise the situation. Questions like:

- How do you think this would work for you?

- What would this strategy deliver?

This helps them clarify their thoughts by rehearsing what they will see, hear, and feel when they are doing this behaviour. Using language like, 'I can't tell you what to do. Only you know what is right for you', will allow them to run a suggestion through their mind and then decide for themselves. It needs to be their idea so get them to come up with solutions and plans for which they can take full ownership.

To influence an Externally referenced salesperson, ask them to consider what other people will see, think and notice. It's useful to know who they use as a reference point, so your understanding of their map of the world will be helpful here. Emphasise what other people think, quote references and statistics and give plenty of feedback.

Sharing examples of successful sales strategies you have observed in others is a great way of providing effective frameworks and approaches to consider. Reports, articles and infographics also work well with Externally referenced salespeople.

Keep in mind. . .

Our preferences are already in place by the time we are seven years old but it's important to remember that they are context/situation dependent.

A significant emotional event has the power to change a salesperson's preference in a given context so always be on the lookout for this when significant things are happening in their personal life.

You are leading a sales team with a range of preferences, which means you are the one that has to adapt if you're to support their development, growth and sales success.

Options/Procedures

American psychologist Frederick Herzberg, who studied motivation, found that too much 'red tape' is likely to cause dissatisfaction. Interestingly, though, he also found that for many people, a lack of process was a problem. This Meta Programme of preferring Options or Procedures relates to the different ways salespeople process their experience and, in particular, whether they need a level of freedom to make choices or feel supported and reassured by a clear sales structure, process or company culture.

Asking a salesperson, 'Why did you choose this job?' will result in one of two types of response. Salespeople with a Procedural preference are likely to tell you the sequence of events that led to them being in the role. They'll share the story of how they were contacted by a recruiter, they liked the sound of the role, went through the interview process, got on well with the people who interviewed them and got the job. Essentially, they will tell you *how* they came to be in the job. Salespeople with an Options preference will tell you the criteria that the role met for them – right industry, location, package, career progression and so on.

Highly Procedural salespeople love to follow a process with precision. They will frequently refer to 'the right way' and 'the wrong way' to do things. For these people, there's a start, middle and an end to every process and, whatever you do, don't attempt to interrupt them when they are in the middle of it because they won't be able to give you their full attention until they've reached the end. They are task driven and can get so caught up in completing a task that they may forget the intended outcome.

Salespeople with an Options preference want the freedom to choose, to experiment and deviate from the process to add variety and flexibility. These salespeople are outcome driven; once the outcome is agreed, they prefer to find their own route to achieving it. They are less likely to follow a process exactly because it's not their natural way.

There is always a sales process to follow but there will be a varying degree of flexibility depending on your organisation, so it's important to understand the implications of this Meta Programme. You are unlikely to be able to get a salesperson with an Options preference to follow the process exactly. Pushing them to do so will crush their creativity and flexibility to go with the flow of a customer. Your salespeople with a Procedural preference will be great at following the sales process every time, but they are usually not as good at dealing with curve balls and adapting the process in the moment to suit the customer or situation. As with all Meta Programmes, there is no right or wrong way to be.

When Procedural-oriented and Options-oriented salespeople get together, there can often be friction. I remember sharing this Meta Programme with a group of salespeople who laughed as they recounted a regular conversation they had in their call centre:

Salesperson O: Yes, I got the sale.

Salesperson P: You did it wrong.

Salesperson O: How could it be wrong when I got the sale?

Salesperson P: You didn't follow the process.

When they understood why this was happening, the friction disappeared.

Process-oriented salespeople don't relish making choices, they just want to stick with the process they know. Options-oriented salespeople need at least the perception of choice. Ensure clarity around the desired outcome and set boundaries for their choices, then let them get on with it. I would recommend giving them two or three options max – too many choices and they won't be able to decide.

The most noticeable traits of someone with an Options preference include:

- Needs choice to stay engaged

- Gets bored with process and goes off course

- Focuses on the outcome rather than the how

- Is flexible in the moment and comfortable deviating from the normal route

- Is creative in generating solutions

- Is not always able to replicate successful strategies that they adopt unconsciously

The most noticeable traits of someone with a Procedural preference include:

- Follows a process exactly once they have it in place – potentially even if it stops being effective

- Needs clarity on each step of the process

- Believes there is a right way and a wrong way

- Is task driven, ticking the box can become the outcome

- Can lose sight of the reason for doing the task

- Can be critical of others not following the process

Influencing strategy

To influence salespeople with a Procedural preference, pay attention to the instructions you give – these should be specific and unambiguous. Tell them that this task has always been done a particular way, that this is 'the right way' to create sales success. They like clear cut steps, preferably ones that are already tried and tested. Bear in mind they are likely to follow the process even when another way might be better.

When influencing salespeople with an Options preference, set parameters, clearly identifying the musts and hard constraints. Offer various possibilities and emphasise they have a choice of route to the desired outcome, then stand back and observe the results.

Keep in mind. . .

Our preferences are already in place by the time we are seven years old but it's important to remember that they are context/situation dependent.

A significant emotional event has the power to change a salesperson's preference in a given context so always be on the lookout for this when significant things are happening in their personal life.

You are leading a sales team with a range of preferences, which means you are the one that has to adapt if you're to support their development, growth and sales success.

Sameness/Difference

When you think about buying new clothes for work, do you think about getting something like you've already got, or about getting something completely different? When you start your working day, do you have a sequence of things you like to do – maybe open your emails first, then your browser and so on? Or do you do whatever pops into your head first and go from there? When a new salesperson joins the team, do you find yourself noticing how similar they are to another person on the team, or do you notice how different this person is? Your answers to these questions will tell you whether you are Sameness- or Difference-oriented.

Ask one of your team, 'How does this role relate to what you were doing five years ago?' When they reply, do they share similarities or differences? When you share information with your sales team, how do they react? Which people accept it and which challenge it? Salespeople with a Sameness preference are more likely to accept and go with the consensus while those with a Difference preference will resist, question and mismatch . . . or even argue. Remember, these patterns aren't good or bad – they just are.

Having a blend of preferences in a sales team is useful because, while consensus is important to a harmonious environment, salespeople with a Difference preference will challenge views and give a valuable new perspective. You will have to accept that they may not agree entirely with any of your suggestions and they are often perceived as argumentative, but they are constantly looking for an alternative view and playing devil's advocate, which can be immensely useful.

A salesperson with a Sameness preference will always be uncomfortable with change and also quite risk averse. They love the status quo. It's important to make them feel safe when things are changing. A salesperson with a Difference preference needs constant variety and challenge to remain engaged. They love new and unique experiences and are much more likely to take risks.

Increase your repertoire as a sales leader – if you tend towards Sameness, learn to value Difference occasionally and challenge ideas and assumptions. Start with your own internal dialogue, it's safer. If you have a Difference preference why not act as if you had a Sameness preference when this might be appropriate – that would be OK, would it not?

The most noticeable traits of a person with a Sameness preference include:

- Habitual behaviour– same outfit, same lunch, same seat every day

- Uncomfortable with change

- Risk averse

- Loves the security of the status quo – a matcher

- Happy to be doing the same thing in the same job for many years

The most noticeable traits of someone with a Difference preference include:

- Needs variety and challenge to keep engaged

- Takes the alternative view – a mismatcher

- Looks for new ways of doing things, even when the old ways are working just fine

- Is more likely to take risks

- Is likely to change jobs or move roles every twelve to twenty-four months if not sufficiently engaged in a role with variety and growth

Influencing strategy

To influence a salesperson with a Sameness preference, when communicating changes frame them as small, gradual and evolutionary. Begin by helping them to identify areas of familiarity or similarity before moving on to the things that will be different – and better. Once they are connected to what will remain the same, they will be better able to digest the things that are changing.

To influence a person with a Difference preference, talk about newness, uniqueness and difference from things they have tried or done before. Introduce commonalities and similarities casually. It's useful to remember that when communicating with a salesperson with this preference, they are likely to counter what you say. A good way to balance this is to start your conversation saying something like, 'You may not agree with this, but. . .' This leaves the person with a challenge: do they challenge the first part or second part of your message? While they try and figure this out, you get more time to get your point across in a way that they are likely to accept.

Keep in mind. . .

Our preferences are already in place by the time we are seven years old but it's important to remember that they are context/situation dependent.

A significant emotional event has the power to change a salesperson's preference in a given context so always be on the lookout for this when significant things are happening in their personal life.

You are leading a sales team with a range of preferences, which means you are the one that has to adapt if you're to support their development, growth and sales success.

Big Picture/Small Details

Imagine you're in a sales meeting talking about your vision and strategy for the new sales year when one of your team interrupts to announce that the CRM won't support your new strategy. You think, 'Why are they mentioning this now? We're talking Big Picture stuff right now; this can wait until we get to the detail.'

Your salespeople all have different needs. Some only want a Big Picture outline of the situation and others want to know, or share, every Small Detail. Some salespeople will emerge from your meetings feeling like you haven't given them enough detail to work with, while others will be frustrated that the meeting dragged on because you were discussing too many finer points.

When you chat with each salesperson, it's important to ascertain how much information they can digest at once, so that you can ensure you craft your communication to get the important points across. This is about the level at which people think. Ask a person with a Big Picture preference, 'How was your holiday?' and they'll respond with something like, 'Great, thanks.' Ask a person with a Small Details preference the same question and you could be there for some time while they describe their journey, the hotel, the weather, the food, the people they met, the shops, what they bought, the journey home and whatever else they think you should know.

When planning as a sales team, it's again useful to have a blend of people with different preferences so that you get the focus on the Big Picture and the Small Details. You'll need to keep to an agenda and set timings, giving the Small Details team the time they need to have their say without getting lost, while not overwhelming the Big Picture people with an information overload. It's a fine balance.

The most noticeable traits of someone with a Big Picture preference include:

- Only interested in topline information
- Will be overwhelmed when presented with too much information
- May deprive others of the information they need
- Is a visionary
- Good at quickly understanding the landscape

The most noticeable traits of someone with a Small Details preference include:

- Goes into lots of detail regardless of how much is needed
- Can lose people without realising
- Good at identifying the small actions required to realise the Big Picture vision
- Needs more time to process their thoughts

- Requires more information to deepen their understanding and do their job

Influencing strategy

It's important to identify the volume of information a salesperson needs in order to perform at their best. Too much detail will overwhelm a salesperson with a Big Picture preference, whereas ambiguity will destabilise one with a Small Details preference. Give each person the level of detail that works for them and check for understanding.

Preferences and leadership

So there you have it, my take on the five most important Meta Programmes to focus on in your efforts to develop and grow each salesperson in your team to increase their success.

Some points to remember when it comes to leading your team:

- While Meta Programme preferences are generally fixed, they are context dependent.

- Significant emotional events have the power to change preferences.

- A preference is neither good nor bad, it is simply a fixed perspective.

- Each preference requires a specific mode of communication.

- Identifying and understanding people's preferences is an essential skill for a sales leader.

- Communicating in a preference-specific way is best for you, for your salespeople, for developing a Growth Mindset and for achieving greater sales success.

Identifying how each of your salespeople view and operate in the world gives you a huge amount of influence. Knowing what makes them tick enables you to ramp up their motivation, increase their self-belief and confidence to step into their Learning Zone and to grow exponentially. This gives you all the ingredients you need to build a high-performing team that is happy, balanced and delivers results.

I cannot stress enough that aligning yourself with each salesperson's preferences will have a hugely positive impact on the results you can deliver as a team, so this is well worth mastering.

TAKE ACTION

It's time to identify the preferences of each of your sales team so that you're can more effectively support and develop them going forward. You'll find a Meta Programme Preference Record in your journal so that you can keep the details at hand until you're fully familiar with each of them.

Be sure to focus on actions that improve your leadership approach with each person, taking into account their preferences, then evaluate the results you see.

It's much easier to focus on one Meta Programme at a time. I would suggest you start with Towards/Away From, as this is the easiest to notice and act on. It's also the one that will have the biggest impact on increasing the motivation in your team.

You can download your Meta Programme spreadsheet to record the preferences of each salesperson in your team at: www.sales-consultancy.com/book-resources

7
Coaching

Coaching is a critical component of sales success. If I'm totally honest, the standard of sales coaching I've observed in sales leaders globally is generally poor. That doesn't mean there aren't some amazing sales leaders out there using coaching to develop their teams and grow their sales, it's just that, in my experience, they are quite rare. I have also observed sales leaders doing their best to support their teams and believing they are coaching them, when in fact they aren't. Why the confusion?

There's a difference between coaching, mentoring and plain old-fashioned telling. It's important to understand which you are doing.

Telling: Telling your salespeople what to do and expecting them to do it.

Mentoring: Teaching them what to do and supporting them in the application of their learning.

Coaching: Asking coaching questions and then listening to the responses. Allowing your salesperson to discover for themselves the best course of action to achieve the desired result. Then supporting their journey of ownership, application and mastery.

A good perspective to keep in mind is that telling teaches your team *what* you want them to think and coaching teaches your team *how* to think for themselves. Be honest, which of these do you do most of the time?

My experience is that most sales leaders are telling or mentoring their salespeople, simply because they've been there, done that and got the T-shirt. What's wrong with this? Your wisdom and experience mean you know exactly what to do next, so why not share it with your sales team to save time and avoid potential disappointment? What's wrong is that you are not developing your people's ability to do things for themselves and, worse, you are killing their confidence to step out of their Comfort Zone and try new things.

If you use a tell or mentor approach with your salespeople most of the time, here are some quick pointers to get you started before we take a deep dive into coaching. These are things you can action immediately:

- Stop telling your team what to do.

- When someone asks you what they should do, reply with 'I have some thoughts, but what do you think?'

- Listen without comment and if they are in the ballpark tell them that sounds like a good plan and to go ahead.

- If they are way off track, ask them, 'What would happen if. . .?' to bring to their attention something important that they have overlooked. Keep going until they come up with a plan that will work.

- Their plan may not be the same as your plan – it doesn't have to be.

- Remember that people will be more motivated to make something a success if it is their plan.

- Your plan will never generate the same level of motivation and ownership so is less likely to succeed – and when it doesn't, they will blame you for its failure.

While this isn't the whole story, it's a good start if you're not currently coaching as much as you could be.

Benefits of sales coaching

According to a *Harvard Business Review* article, good quality coaching can improve sales performance by up to 19%.[11] What is particularly interesting, though, is that this stat doesn't apply to your entire team. Remember the 10–80–10 rule from Chapter 2? Your top 10% are already performing at their best, so coaching them won't lead to massive gains. Your bottom 10% need to decide whether to save themselves or leave. They need to make that decision before coaching can have any impact. It's those salespeople in the middle 80% where your big wins will come. First, it's your biggest group; second, they have a desire to create more success; and third, they aren't quite there yet and need your coaching to get there.

Here are some more stats published by the Center for Sales Strategy,[12] which make for compelling reading:

- Companies with dynamic sales coaching programmes achieve 28% higher win rates.

- Companies that provide quality coaching can reach 7% greater annual revenue growth.

---

11 M Dixon and B Adamson, *The Dirty Secret of Effective Sales Coaching* (Harvard Business Review, January 31, 2011), https://hbr.org/2011/01/the-dirty-secret-of-effective

12 S Smith, *7 Sales Coaching Statistics All Sales Leaders Need to See* (the Centre for Sales Strategy, 2020), https://blog.thecenterforsalesstrategy.com/sales-coaching-statistics-all-sales-leaders-need-to-see

- As many as 60% of sales reps say they're more likely to leave their job if their manager is a poor coach. More than two-thirds of employees reporting to a manager who is not a good coach consider quitting their jobs.

- Sales reps getting thirty minutes or less of sales coaching per week have a win rate of 43%, whereas those that receive at least two hours of coaching per week, have a win rate of 56%.

- Sales coaching and mentoring is cited as the most important role played by frontline managers, according to 74% of leading companies.

- Companies with a formal coaching process see 91.2% overall quota attainment, compared to 84.7% in companies with an informal coaching process.

- The forecast deals win rate for companies whose managers spent more time on coaching than selling is 8.2% higher, and overall revenue attainment is 5.2% higher.

The most common improvements I've observed when sales leaders start effectively coaching are:

- Their team start solving their own problems

- Sales skills improve

- Conversion rates increase

- Impact of the sales induction increases, so new salespeople start generating sales more quickly

- Helps the leader and their team grow and develop

- Increases confidence, proactivity and wellbeing

- Improves sales results

Coaching has a massive impact on the wellbeing of your sales team and how they feel when they are working, which results in more engaged, happy and successful salespeople. In summary, you should definitely be coaching your team, especially your 80% salespeople.

Getting started

In this chapter, I'm going to dive into the GROW coaching model created by Sir John Whitmore.[13] It is easy to apply, widely written about and you can find lots of free resources online. You may even find online courses to support your coaching development.

The most important thing is to practise your coaching approach with your salespeople. The more time you spend doing this, the faster you will get to mastery. You can read about coaching, you can watch videos about coaching, but you won't become a great coach until you coach. The best coaching practice you will ever get is the coaching you do with your salespeople. By observing the impact you have, tweaking and perfecting your approach, you will soon become a master of sales

---

13   J Whitmore, *Coaching for Performance* (Nicholas Brealey, 1992)

coaching. Because all your team are different, you will be constantly learning and broadening your skills.

Treat this chapter on coaching as a starting point. If you are already coaching your sales team, I hope you will find a few pointers that enhance what you're already doing.

The GROW coaching model

GROW stands for:

- Goal

- Reality

- Options

- Will/Way forward

As a coach, you have a role in each of these areas:

- **Goal**: Help each salesperson clarify their goals in a specific area of focus/topic. These can be short-term or long-term goals.

- **Reality**: Help each salesperson get clarity around what is happening right now, including any obstacles, and allow them to find their own insights.

- **Options:** Help them identify and evaluate the different options open to them.

- **Will/Way forward**: Help them determine the way forward and assess what they are willing to commit to doing and by when.

It's so important when coaching a member of your team that you start by asking what their goal or objective is and then actively listening to their response. And I mean really listening. That doesn't include you plotting your approach to get them on the shortest path from A to B. That doesn't include you judging their goal. That doesn't include you hoping that it doesn't take too long.

It means emptying yourself of everything. Imagine your body is a laptop – you need to shut down all the programmes so nothing is running in the background, you're just switched on. No judging. No plotting. No planning. Just listening. Briefly note down anything you want to return to. If you make too many notes, you won't be listening.

Maintain eye contact and keep facial expressions neutral. No eyebrow raises. No looks of approval, no looks of disapproval. This is not as easy as it sounds and will take some practice. Remember that your expressions communicate your inner reactions and thoughts and can unconsciously influence your salesperson down your desired avenue. That doesn't help them and it definitely doesn't help you to develop that person beyond where they currently are. Rapport and psychological safety are crucial to create a safe space for them to speak openly. What gets said in the session must stay in the session and not be repeated elsewhere unless agreed.

Once you have established the goal, don't get hung up on sticking rigidly to the order of the GROW model. You can go with the flow of your salesperson's responses – you may find you meander around the sections because that's the way their thoughts are flowing. As long as you cover each point and close the session with actions to take moving forward, that's fine.

Your skill in covering each element of the GROW model will increase the more coaching you do. The quality of your questions and your ability to actively listen without judgement will determine the success of the session. It's also useful to remember that you don't always need a formal coaching session – you can use coaching questions in the moment. Whenever you notice an opportunity to coach, step up and go for it.

Tears are not an uncommon reaction in a coaching session. This is not a bad thing. It shows that you have built a deep level of rapport with your salesperson and have created a space of psychological safety where they feel safe to let their guard down and freely express themselves. Always be sure to have water and tissues available when coaching face to face so that you don't have to leave the person alone. If they get embarrassed, reassure them that tears are a good thing – it means that they are ready to let go of whatever it is that's been inside them. Encourage them to share their emotions, listen and stay neutral.

Don't try and stop them from crying or sharing. This will cause them to push down whatever it is they need to release. This is an unhealthy outcome as the issue will continue to plague them, and you. If you're uncomfortable with tears, you'll have to connect with your heart and get comfortable. It's part of being a great leader. You must be able to hold the space when one of your team is upset.

GROW coaching question bank

Here are some coaching questions for each element of the GROW model to get you started. Feel free to add to this list and adapt it to your personality and to the personalities and Meta Programmes of your salespeople.

Goal:

- What goal do you want to achieve?

- What would you like to have happen?

- What do you really want?

- What would you like to accomplish?

- What result are you trying to achieve?

- What do you want to achieve?

- What outcome would be ideal for you?

- What do you want to change?

- What is your outcome for achieving this goal?

- What would the benefits be if you achieved this goal?

Reality:

- What is happening now (what, who, when and how often)?

- What is the effect or result of this?

- What steps have you already taken toward what you want?

- How would you describe what you did?

- Where are you now in relation to your goal?

- On a scale of 1 to 10, where are you? (Give them the criteria for a 1 and a 10.)

- What has contributed to your success so far?

- What progress have you made so far?

- What is working well for you right now?

- What stops you achieving what you want?

- What stops you?

- What do you think is really happening?

- Who do you know who has achieved this goal?

- What could you learn from them?

- What have you already tried?

- How could you turn this around?

- What could you do better next time?

- If you asked X, what would they say about you?

- On a scale of 1 to 10, how severe/serious/urgent is the situation? (Again, give the criteria for a 1 and a 10.)

- If someone said/did that to you, what would you think/feel/do?

Options:

- What are your options?

- What do you think you need to do next?

- What could be your first step?

- What do you think you need to do to get a better result (or get closer to your goal)?

- What else could you do?

- Who else might be able to help?

- What would happen if you did nothing?

- What has worked for you already? How could you do more of that?

- What would happen if you did that?

- What is the hardest/most challenging part of that for you?

- What advice would you give to a friend about that?

- What would you gain/lose by doing/saying that?

- If someone did/said that to you, what do you think would happen?

- What is the best/worst thing about that option?

- Which option do you feel ready to act on?

- How have you tackled this/a similar situation before?

- What could you do differently?

- Who do you know who has encountered a similar situation?

- If anything were possible, what would you do?

- What would you do if you were totally confident in succeeding?

- What else?

Will/way forward:

- What do you think you need in order to do this right now?

- How are you going to do that?

- How will you know when you have achieved it?

- What obstacles could get in the way of your success?

- What contingencies do you need to plan for?

- What could be missing?

- What one small step will you take now?

- When are you going to start?

- How will you know you have been successful?

- What support do you need to get that done?

- What will happen if you don't do this?

- What is the cost of you not doing this?

- What do you need from me/others to help you achieve this?

- What three actions can you take this week?

- On a scale of 1 to 10, how committed/motivated are you to taking these actions?

- What would make it a 10?

 You can download these questions here: www.sales-consultancy.com/book-resources

Use the questions that you need in the moment, the ones that create the biggest awareness for your salesperson. These questions are just examples and variations, not a list to ask in one session. If you have good rapport, you can trust your instincts. If it feels right, go ahead and ask. If it feels clunky or uncomfortable, ask something that's a better fit for the moment. Having said that, sometimes the best question to ask your salesperson may feel slightly uncomfortable for you, especially if you're new to coaching. Check in with yourself. Are you avoiding a question simply because of your own 'stuff'? If that's the case, seek out somebody who can help you overcome your issues around it.

TAKE ACTION

It's time to think about what actions you're going to take to improve your coaching skills.

Be sure to focus on actions that will improve your coaching and sales leadership skills to help you develop a strong Sales Growth Mindset Coaching Culture.

Start by doing some touchline coaching in its easiest form every day, to practise and integrate the skills required. You can then move on to formal, one-to-one coaching sessions with each member of your team.

8
Tough Love

One of the most common avoidances I see when working with sales leaders – and this is globally – is the tricky conversation. I'm talking about those Tough Love conversations that you know deep down need to be had, yet they rarely happen. Why? Because nobody wants to deliver challenging news or feedback that may upset someone. They often believe it's kinder to avoid a direct conversation and hope the person figures it out for themselves, or maybe hears it from someone else. They don't want to be the culprit. They think it's better to be quiet and kind.

The irony is that, in leaving these words unspoken, that member of your team is left in blissful ignorance to continue doing whatever it is they are doing. Others may notice they are doing it too and start talking about them.

How is letting that happen kind? It's not – it's cruel.
You're not giving them the opportunity to change. It is
taking the easy route rather than the right one.

Failure to have difficult conversations is a widespread
weakness in sales leadership that has severe
consequences over time. So what's it going to be? Easy,
cruel and weak or the right, courageous and kind action?
There really is only one choice.

How to get started

At first, nobody relishes having these conversations
but there are things you can do to ease yourself into it
gently, build your 'tough love' muscles and increase your
skills over time.

Be quick

Have the conversation as soon as you become aware of
something that needs to be addressed, but don't act on
someone else's account of something that happened as
if it were fact. If you have heard about the behaviour
from someone else rather than witnessed it yourself,
treat their account as a starting point. You could then
observe the person involved more closely to ascertain
whether what you've been told is true, or maybe you
could have an exploratory conversation to establish
their perspective on what happened. You can't have
a Tough Love conversation unless and until you've

witnessed the issue yourself or confirmed something to be true, but you need to act quickly regardless.

Get in the right mindset

When you have a potentially difficult conversation, you need to come from a place of kindness and curiosity. If you're feeling negative emotions about the person or are making judgements around the issue, do not have the conversation just yet. Use TFAR to tweak your trigger thought and feelings so that you can have a neutral conversation.

Plan your opening minute

When you deliver the first minute with a confident and kind or neutral tone, you start the conversation off with a beautiful flow that is easy to maintain. Once you've planned your opening, practise, practise and practise – then practise some more. Record yourself and listen to how you sound. Imagine being on the receiving end – what impact would that opening have on you? Keep tweaking it until you feel good saying it and hearing it and you absolutely know that it conveys kindness and compassion.

Be open and allow unfolding

After your opening, things will unfold in their own way. You have no control, which means you need to be totally present in order to take in everything that's being said. Don't do any mental preparation of how you are going to respond, simply listen and respond in the moment. Be prepared for emotions, maybe even tears – as with coaching sessions, should somebody get upset, allow them to do so safely and with support. Simply sit quietly, hold the space and listen. The release of tears shows huge trust and psychological safety and is a positive step towards resolving the issue.

Be kind

Being kind doesn't mean being soft or dishonest. Telling someone that everything is OK when it's not, is not kind. Being kind in the context of difficult conversations is about delivering potentially uncomfortable information with kindness and compassion, taking the other person's map of the world into consideration and tailoring your delivery so that they hear your message in the most digestible way. You should aim to communicate this news in a way that creates hope and empowers them to make better choices. Remind them that you are on their side, you are their sales leader, you want them to succeed. That energy has to come through.

Having shared these pointers, I'm now going to give you a more detailed framework that you can use for constructive Tough Love conversations. Ones that make you feel like you've done a great job and make your salesperson feel supported and empowered going forward. This is the best and fastest route to a healthy and successful sales culture.

Tough love framework

There are four phases in this framework.

1. Your opening

2. Their response

3. Resolution plan

4. Joint reviews

The first phase you can prepare and practise ahead of time. The subsequent phases roll out as they will, but you can do some prep to ensure your thoughts are in the right place. The following sections will outline the actions required in each phase.

1. Your opening

- Describe the issue, situation and/or behaviour, as you see it.

- Give specific examples to demonstrate what you mean.

- Describe how it makes you and/or others feel.

GROW YOUR PEOPLE GROW YOUR SALES

- Share why it is important to resolve the issue/ situation. What are the consequences? What's at stake?

- Identify your contribution to the problem. What did you do or not do that contributed to this situation?

- Indicate your desire to resolve the issue/situation.

2. Their response

- Invite the other person to share their views, emotions and perceptions without interruption.

- Listen carefully and check for full understanding – don't be satisfied by superficial or glib responses.

- Acknowledge their feelings and ask questions.

- Keep the conversation on track. Don't let it get hijacked by other matters or old grievances.

3. Resolution plan

- Explore the options that address the most important concerns and help achieve the agreed outcome.

- Discuss what is needed for you both to be satisfied.

- Check if anything has been left unsaid that needs to be shared.

- Summarise your understanding of the outcomes and ask the other person to do the same.

- Be clear about next steps.

- Agree when you will get together to review actions and progress and put this in both of your calendars.

4. Joint reviews

- Review the issue/situation/behaviour together.

- What have you each learned?

- What will you each do differently going forward to maintain positive behaviour and mindset?

This framework isn't cast in stone, it's a general guide to each phase of a Tough Love conversation with a salesperson to keep you both on track and moving towards a positive outcome for all concerned.

TAKE ACTION

It's time to think about what Tough Love conversations you might have been putting off. Which of these conversations can you have now that you have a framework to support you?

Be sure to focus on actions that improve your ability to have these meaningful conversations that have such a positive impact on creating a Sales Growth Mindset Culture.

Go for the easiest Tough Love conversation first – it's always good to practice by addressing a simple issue before tackling the more challenging conversations.

9
Getting To Know Your Salespeople

Cast your mind back to Chapter 2 when I introduced the 10–80–10 rule. In this chapter you're going to take a deeper dive into your 80% salespeople. I'm going to share a process I use with all my clients to assess the landscape of each member of a team and, more importantly, how you can navigate that landscape to improve their skills, mindset and sales.

First, a quick reminder of the 10–80–10 rule: roughly 10% of your team are top performers and will be regardless of the quality of leadership, because they rarely need it. They are already aligned to your corporate values, are generally outcome focused and have a Growth Mindset.

Roughly another 10% of your team are under-performers. They tend to have a Fixed Mindset, and no matter how you try to help them, for various reasons it never works out.

Then there's roughly 80% of your team who are somewhere in the middle. They have good months and bad months; they can hit targets but rarely exceed them, even though they have the capacity to.

Now it's time to evaluate your team. Remember that the biggest revenue generators may not be in your top 10% if they are not aligned with your core values or use inappropriate behaviour to achieve those sales. These guys still need development so fall under your 80% category. You true top 10% will only need a regular check in, maybe some positive reinforcement, or sometimes nothing at all. Don't interfere, just let them get on with what they do best.

Your bottom 10% need to decide what they want. Have they already checked out or do they want to stay and commit? Only they can decide. You cannot save them, so don't try – you will only be prolonging the pain for everyone concerned.

Now you're left with your 80% salespeople. This is where the gold is. These are the members of your team that want to do better, do more and be more. They just can't do it on their own. They need a leader who can develop them through small, digestible changes. A leader who can identify what they need from moment to moment. Is it a little nudge, or a little lift? You have to gauge the amount of pressure to exert – just enough to grow them, not enough to crush their confidence.

The 80% reality check

Once you have identified your 80%, the first thing you need to do is a reality check on each person. This will give you a better understanding of the landscape you are navigating. Below is my formula for uncovering what's 'real' about that person. Feel free to add questions relevant to your organisation or sector:

- What's the truth?

- What are your mind reads or assumptions?

- What can be changed?

- What's fixed and needs a workaround or acceptance?

If you're going to support, develop and grow the 80% members of your sales team, you will need to create a plan for each person. First, you must separate the facts from assumptions and mind reads. Once you have the facts, you can create the plan. Establish the following for each person:

- Their sales performance against targets.

- How aligned are they with your core values?

- How aligned are they to your sales processes?

- How do they interact with other members of your team and other supporting departments in the business?

- What are they good at that brings value?

- What weaknesses interfere with their performance?

  - Can they be improved or are they fixed parts of their personality?

  - Do they have a desire and willingness to improve?

- What is their map of the world?

  - Towards or Away From

  - Internal or External

  - Options or Procedural

  - Sameness or Difference

  - Big Picture or Small Details

  - Motivations and drivers

  - Values, both career and personal

  - Beliefs, positive and negative, about themselves and others

  - Family life

  - Personal habits and hobbies

- How often are they in The Valley of Reasons and Excuses?

    - When in The Valley, how long do they stay there?

- Do they leave their general personal life outside of work, or does it interfere with their work?

- Are there any significant personal/family issues that need to be taken into consideration?

- Is there anything else you know about them that could have an impact on their sales performance?

You can download the 80% Reality Check Framework here: www.sales-consultancy.com/book-resources

The way I like to work through this reality check with my clients is to write responses on post-it notes and spread them out on a wall. Then I split them into two categories:

1. Facts

2. Assumptions/mind reads

Facts

When I've got all the 'fact' post-its, I split them further into the following categories:

- Strengths

- Weaknesses

- That can be improved
- That are fixed and require workarounds or acceptance

- Meta Programme preferences and personal traits
- Values, motivations and drivers

When you have categorised your facts, you can start formulating a development plan. First off, you can park the strengths because these are already working their magic. You may need to call on them to leverage other aspects of your plan, but for now you're going to focus on the weaknesses that can be improved, taking the other facts into consideration.

For example, if your salesperson isn't great at building new customer relationships, this is a fixable issue.

You should take into consideration:

- Their beliefs about themselves, your customers, your products/services and any other relevant factors.
- Their skills.
- Are they Towards or Away From? This will determine your approach.
- Other psychological preferences that are relevant to this weakness.
- Any other facts you have identified that could influence their behaviour, your approach to

developing them and the starting point you're working from.

Once you've considered all the facts you can weigh up your options and create a plan that really helps your salesperson develop, grow and succeed.

Going through this exercise even once should help you begin to get a sense of the uniqueness of every member of your team and why they need a specific, tailored approach to their development. It takes time and effort on your part to complete an effective Reality Check that not only informs you but benefits the person you are leading.

Before you go full pelt into stamping out every last weakness in your salesperson – stop. The most important rule – and yes, it is a rule – is that you must address one weakness at a time. This ensures that all their energy, and your support, is laser focused. When your focus is spread across too many things, the energy dissipates, reducing the potential for successful and positive change.

What you are aiming to create in your salesperson is a more helpful mindset that generates the behaviours that will boost their performance. Choose one weakness, the one that, if eliminated, will have the biggest and most profound positive impact on their mindset and performance. Once you see evidence of a shift in mindset and positive results you can move on to the next most impactful weakness. It's a simple and beautiful process. All the while, your salesperson is growing in confidence, self-belief and happiness – and you already know that happier salespeople generate 37% more sales.

Do this with every single person in your 80% category and don't be surprised if some of these rise to the top and enter your top 10%. Once you open their minds, anything is possible. This process never ends; you should always be doing this for your 80% people, whoever they are.

Assumptions and mind reads

These need further investigation or evidence. If you find that most of your post-its (or however else you recorded your responses) are in this category, then you haven't yet got everything you need to create a plan. You've been leading based on assumptions, which will limit your ability to improve your team and sales. However, this realisation is itself something to celebrate because addressing this going forward will have a positive impact on sales. You're no longer in the dark, no longer unknowing, no longer pondering why. Now you can do something about it.

Moving from assumptions to facts can be as simple as having conversations with others in your organisation, with the salesperson direct or with your customers (discreetly). What you are looking for is examples, not opinions. Once you have examples of behaviours and events from which you can establish facts, you can move on to creating your plan.

Your plan

Once you've established which weakness you're going to address first you have two choices, depending on the context of all the facts you've uncovered in your reality check:

1. Use the GROW coaching model from Chapter 7

2. Navigating a Tough Love conversation from Chapter 8

I would generally opt for coaching, though there are situations when it could be less effective. For example, when you have a high-revenue salesperson with a poor attitude perhaps not aligned with the core values of the business, a Tough Love conversation might be the best option. Trust your instincts and give it a go. The worst thing that could happen is that things don't go according to plan and you have to try an alternative approach – as per the Five Keys to Sales Leadership Success discussed in Chapter 2.

TAKE ACTION

It's time to think about your next steps towards completing your Reality Checks. Which of your team will you start with?

Be sure to focus on facts and examples that improve your clarity and understanding so that you can develop the 80% salespeople in your team, generate increased sales success and create a healthy Sales Growth Mindset Culture.

Again, go for the quick wins first. This will help you to become more proficient at separating facts from assumptions before you move on to the more challenging Reality Checks later on.

10
Sales And Spirituality

There is a part of me that I rarely talk about in my work yet is present in every part of it, and the rest of my life too. My spirituality.

At the age of five, my Italian parents sent me to a Roman Catholic school run by nuns. My first teacher was the kindest, gentlest and most beautiful nun who made me feel safe despite me not wanting to be there and not speaking a word of English. It's a good job I was a fast learner.

It was in those early years that I learned about God and began to chat with him. I would share all kinds of things with God – my day, my dreams, my desires, my fears. . . everything. He was like my best friend, who I couldn't see but always knew in my heart was listening. I was never one of those kids that knelt at the side of the bed praying. My conversations with God were, and still are, more of a 'drop in when I need a chat' kind of thing.

At thirteen I fell out of love with religion and stopped going to church but continued talking with God. He was like a counsellor, listening and never judging. I had most of my best ideas while chatting with him. I say 'chat', I was pretty much doing all the talking. When great things happened in my life, I thanked him. When sad or bad things happened in my life, I would ask him for strength. When I was twenty-three my boyfriend ended our relationship just three months before our wedding. I was devastated. I hadn't been to church for ten years but in my lunch break I walked to Westminster Cathedral in London and sat and cried. I shared my sadness and grief with God and I asked him, if this was for the best, to please give me the strength and courage to get through it. It was indeed the best thing for us both.

Why am I sharing this with you in a book about sales leadership? Because my beliefs and conversations with God have influenced how I am in the world, how I show up as a human being, how I treat others. That, for me, has been the backbone of my success in sales, sales leadership and sales development. As a salesperson, I cared about every prospect and customer, unconditionally. It didn't matter if it was a small sale, huge sales or no sale. I cared for them all the same and wanted to do the best thing for them. I saw sales as a huge act of service and I still do. It has been a beautiful and honourable way to spend my life.

As a new sales manager, I added 'caring about my team' to my remit. When my lack of experience and impact meant that I wasn't as good a sales leader as I wanted to be, my belief drove me to learn from others. I consumed information and knowledge from every source I could get my hands on. There was no internet back then, so it was books and audio programmes. This led me down the path of psychology and a career in mindset development, which was totally aligned with my spirituality.

Now, as a sales trainer and enabler I care about every single person on our programmes, whether live, virtual or on our eLearning platform. It's about giving each person the best learning experience and making them feel good about themselves (and others) in the process.

Of course you can be successful without believing in God, many people are, but for me there's a quality that comes from spirituality and the associated values that makes success more aligned to the benefit of all.

There is a mantra I live by that guides all of my decisions:

'Is it good for me, is it good for others and is it good for the planet?'

You may not consider yourself spiritual, but you may find that some of the values I live by that support my success are values that you share.

My values

These can change over time, but most are a constant that I live by in my life as a whole:

- Presence
- Allowing unfolding
- Openness
- Faith
- Focus
- Love

These are the words I use to describe my values. When I share what they mean to me, you may find you have similar values that you call something else.

Below is what these values mean to me and how I apply them in the context of sales leadership.

Presence

For me, presence is about being completely with the person or people I'm communicating with in that moment, being totally available to them in all senses. This means not thinking about what I'm going to say next. Not drifting off to what I'll be doing later. Not judging them or what they say. Not doing anything at all but being with them in the moment.

In sales leadership, being present means you have a better understanding of the landscape you are navigating. You take in more information and can make better and wiser choices. You can't truly listen while your mind is working things out, planning or judging. Presence is not something you can fake or do half-hearted. You're either present or you're not. Your presence allows the other person to share their truth, how they experience things. Without their truth, you haven't got a starting point. If you want to get from A to B in the shortest possible time, you must join them at their A. Unless you are there with them, they'll be left feeling unheard and uncared for.

Allowing unfolding

For me, this means that I don't push, or pull. I let things unfold at the pace that's right for all concerned. My experience tells me that everything unfolds perfectly when you ask the right questions, do the right things and take the best actions for all involved.

In sales leadership, pushing your salespeople to close sales that aren't ready to be closed means you're stuck in your own map. If your customer isn't ready, they aren't ready, regardless of the pressure you put on them. Nobody likes pressure and people will push back, which endangers the relationship and shows a lack of understanding. Don't push or pressurise your salespeople – this creates an unhealthy culture that breeds unhelpful behaviours like lies, deceit, resignation and more. You'll be stamping out the magic that grows your sales.

Pressure is not the same as nudging your salesperson out of their Comfort Zone in order to support and develop them. This is vital for their growth. Considered nudges into the Learning Zone create growth. Pushing and pressure inhibit growth. Don't be a hard, tough or deluded bully, be a caring realist who knows when to nudge for the benefit of all – and when not to.

Openness

For me, openness is about being curious and open to other possibilities to uncover interesting perspectives and opportunities that I may not have come up with myself. Because I've been in the game for a long time, it would be easy for me to stick with what has worked for me in the past. Yes, these methods may still work but the world is constantly evolving and so must I – while something may still work, it may not be the best solution.

In sales leadership, being a 'know it all' style leader is an easy way to erode confidence in your team. They will either feel that they can't ever be as good as you or that you always interfere. You want salespeople that think for themselves, that are able to assess situations in the moment, not ask what you want them to do. Having an open, sharing culture leads to creativity and ideas that you may not have come up with alone. Use your expertise to facilitate and coach your team to come up with new and better ideas. Be open to their suggestions and praise their contribution, even if it's not what you decide to do as a team going forward. Keep the creative juices flowing.

Faith

For me, this is about having faith that everything will work out in the end, in the right way for all involved. If I am meant to have something in my life and I take the required action, it will be so. If it's not meant to be, then it won't be – no matter what action I take. Then I trust that something better is on its way. This stops me getting attached to 'stuff' and 'outcomes', freeing me to show up as my best self, devoid of the negative emotions associated with disappointment.

In sales leadership, knowing that there is a bigger game being played over which you have no control not only keeps you sharp, open and curious, it also enables greater relaxation and flexibility when faced with challenging situations. You also start to look for the best in people and become more forgiving, kind and supportive with your team. Not knowing whether a team member could be your next superstar, your lowest performer, a strong anchor or just visiting for a short time adds to the adventure and the grounded realism.

Get comfortable with not knowing – the unknown is one of your best friends. Faith, or belief – whatever that means for you – enables you to show up in this state of unknowing as your best self and do something great.

Focus

For me, being present, open, allowing unfolding with faith are the forerunners to laser-focused action. Being able to do the right thing, at the right time and in the right way requires focus. It's about making things happen with full knowledge of the landscape I'm navigating and the wisdom required to do the right thing for each person in my team or on my programmes.

In your sales leadership, I'm sure that you already have focus – but are you focusing on the right thing? It's easy to get caught up in stories, your own and/or those of others, that influence your thoughts and actions.

Below is a LinkedIn post from my friend Marcus Cauchi that highlights a great example of focus without wisdom:

> **Sales leader:** Your revenues are excellent. You're sitting at what, 220% of quota?

Salesperson: Yes.

Sales leader: Good job. I am concerned that you aren't sending out enough proposals though.

Salesperson: I don't understand.

Sales leader: Our VC and the board want everyone to be sending out at least fifteen proposals per month.

Salesperson: Why?

Sales leader: Because more proposals mean more sales.

Salesperson: They do?

Sales leader: It stands to reason.

Salesperson: Does it really? Forgive my naivety but I was under the impression I'm producing more than anyone else in our team?

Sales leader: You are.

Salesperson: And my proposal to closed order ratio stands at 92%.

Sales leader: Yes.

Salesperson: And you want to distract me from what is clearly working by writing more proposals?

Thought bubble: *To satisfy the whims of a bunch of bankers and an investor who never sold a thing in their life.*

Sales leader: Yes.

Salesperson: Really?

Thought bubble: *Having money doesn't make you an expert in what customers need to buy from us. And the fact that you've even brought this up gives me cause for concern that you, sir, are an idiot.*

Sales leader: Yes. I'm getting pressure from above to get more proposals out of the door.

If you think I'm exaggerating, I've had something similar to this conversation at least a dozen times this past year. It is symptomatic of why sales has taken a wrong turn. Just because you can, doesn't mean you should!'[14]

Focused? YES. Wise? NO.

---

14 M Cauchi, www.linkedin.com/feed/update/urn:li:activi ty:6785824819255508992

Don't fall into the trap of a good story. Yes, more proposals probably do lead to more sales when a salesperson is not a top performer and it should be part of their development process to get them doing more of the right things. But when you have a top performer, they are like a finely tuned athlete. They are a master of their craft and can create magic on their own. Sometimes they don't know exactly how they do it, it's become an unconscious behaviour over time – tinker with that recipe at your peril.

Love

For me, my starting point is always to come from my heart space, with love. This is where kindness, compassion and forgiveness sit. In this sense, love is about knowing that everyone is on a unique journey – I am joining them on theirs and they are joining me on mine. What kind of travelling companion am I going to be? Coming from a space of love means that I keep their welfare at heart and take the best action for their personal growth so that they can shine more brightly.

In sales leadership, coming from your heart space when building your salespeople's confidence and self-belief, nudging them into their Learning Zone, supporting them in times of challenge, challenging them at times of inaction and having Tough Love conversations will always lead to better results. If you come from a place of wanting to do the best for them – not dissimilar to the way a parent does for their child – you are unlikely to go wrong. The opposite of love is not hate, it's indifference. When you become indifferent to your team, they can feel that you no longer care.

Don't let your ego get in the way. The moment you put yourself before your team, you are all doomed. Coming from a place of love doesn't mean that you have to love everyone. It simply means that your actions come from your heart and are more likely to have a positive impact. Over time, you will find that love conquers all.

These are my values and how they translate to sales leadership. I'm sure you will be doing some of these things already and perhaps have your own names for them – you'll normally find that you feel great about yourself and your team when you're doing them. Think about how you can incorporate more of these behaviours into your leadership to develop a happy and healthy sales culture. Be warned: they are not actions that you can learn, they are philosophies and values that you manifest through your actions. The actions on their own do not have the same power.

TAKE ACTION

This has been quite a different chapter and you may want to approach what you do next differently.

I would recommend you take some quiet time to reflect on your own values, the things that allow you to show up as your best self. If you're feeling stuck, ask yourself, 'What would my best self do right now?' Write down your values in your journal so that you can continually remind yourself and refer back to as your overarching guide.

This part of the work is a slow burn, the long game. It will unfold over time and, if you're up for it, the rewards far outweigh the effort of making changes.

Decide for yourself how you want to do this and commit to five minutes every day where you think about your approach. Your journey will start to evolve from your daily practice of contemplation.

Take gentle steps to improve or increase your actions, aligned with your values, that create a happy and healthy Sales Growth Mindset Culture.

11
Your Leadership Journey

We've reached the final chapter – so what's next?

There are a number of ways you could have read this book:

- You read straight through without taking any action with the intention of doing that later. . . and still haven't.

- You read straight through with the intention of going through again and taking action after each chapter.

- You took action after reading each chapter.

- A mix of the above.

Whatever your way is, a few things will be useful to know going forward. First, it's impossible to implement everything in this book quickly and make a positive impact. Second, cut yourself some slack and be kind to yourself if you've done little or nothing at all. Beating yourself up gets you nowhere. Third, it's much more effective to pick one or two concepts that really resonate with you and implement them until you are totally comfortable and making an impact, before going onto the next one. Slow but sure progress always outperforms fast and thoughtless.

Finally, you will have long established habits, the ways you currently do things, which will need recalibrating. Don't give yourself a hard time if you slip back into old habits in the early days, this is part of your evolution. If you focus, you will become more aware of when you're slipping and eventually, you'll find yourself implementing your new habits naturally and with ease. Nevertheless, there may be some quick wins available to you if you're already part way there. If this applies, start there to make fast inroads – it always feels good to see changes in mindset and behaviours, both yours and your team's. Keep in mind that your biggest wins will be with your 80% team members, so any concepts that will support their growth are worth prioritising.

At this point, I'll remind you of the seven-step process I introduced in Chapter 1, which can support and guide you in implementing all of the other processes, approaches and actions discussed in this book:

1. **Think** about the impact you want before taking any action.

2. **Assess** your inner state – are there any negative emotions coursing through your veins?

3. **Shift** into neutral and detach yourself from any negative emotions.

4. **Establish** the best outcome for all concerned.

5. **Consider** the people involved – how do you need to communicate so that they will hear you?

6. **Take action** and observe the impact of your communication to ensure it's being received in a way that achieves your desired outcome.

7. **Change** what you are doing if it's not working.

Making every day count

There are a number of small daily habits you can implement that have an immediate positive impact. These are easy but take consistent effort, and include:

- Morning check-ins with each person in your team

    - How are they feeling?

    - What do they need to be in the best mindset possible?

    - How did yesterday go?

- What are their actions and priorities for today?

- What can you do to leave them feeling uplifted?

- Praise their application of new skills, even if they are not achieving the ideal outcome

- Use on-the-spot coaching for any challenges they are experiencing

- Coach anyone who is resisting necessary activities to establish what the barrier is

- Observe your team in action as often as possible

  - Are they incorporating positive behaviours?

  - What do you notice in their attitude?

  - What are they doing well?

  - What are their areas of development?

  - Give positive and developmental feedback on their activity

- Check in with each member of your team at the end of their day

  - How has their day gone?

  - How are they feeling about their successes and challenges of the day?

  - What have they learned today that they can take into tomorrow to achieve more success?

  - How can you make sure they end their day in a positive state of mind?

The development process

Development is a journey, a process that happens over time. Expecting your people to get things right first time is unrealistic and leads to disappointment, judgement and blame. It's much healthier to allow them to work through this process in their own time. Remember that they are all at different chapters in their career and someone further on will have more resources to move them through the process at a faster pace. Regardless of pace, the process will look roughly similar for everyone:

Step 1: Learn

Your salesperson learns something new.

Step 2: Action

They incorporate their new approach into their working day while you provide coaching support, feedback and observations. It will probably be a bit clunky at first while they get comfortable with it. I always suggest they test an approach at least three times before deciding what to tweak. Make only one tweak at a time – more than this stops you identifying which change has made the biggest contribution to the outcome.

Step 3: Master

As your salesperson becomes more relaxed with their new approach, their personality will start to shine through and add its own magic. Encourage, support and coach them through this part of the process to perfect the new approach and make it their own.

And that's it. With this, you have everything you need to create a happy and healthy Sales Growth Mindset Culture. Now it's up to you. This can't happen without your input. You are the leader and you're in control of the game.

I'll leave you with some wise words from Matthew Syed's book, *Bounce:*[15]

> 'Excellence is about striving for what is just out of reach and not quite making it. It is about grappling with tasks beyond current limitations and falling short again and again. The paradox of excellence is that it is built upon the foundations of necessary failure.'

TAKE ACTION

This is a book that you can read time and time again. Each time you do, you'll get something new from it because you will always be starting from a new

---

15 M Syed, *Bounce* (Fourth Estate, 2011)

standpoint. You will have developed because of what you have read, what you have implemented and the results you have experienced. This creates wisdom. The wiser you get, the deeper you can go.

You can also use this book as a reference. Dive into whatever chapter you need in the moment, and return to the journal you've kept along the way, adding new insights as they occur. I'm so thrilled that you chose me to be part of your sales leadership development journey and I look forward to hearing your success stories. You can share them here: www.sales-consultancy.com/ book-resources

---

Now, though, it is time to think about your next steps. What will these be? How can you serve your team by stepping up as a sales leader and going beyond where you have been until now?

You get to choose, so choose wisely.

Acknowledgements

I am so grateful to everyone who has supported me in the writing of this book.

A special mention to the lovely people who reviewed my manuscript – Ben Gaston, Christopher Capon, Samantha Logue, Sarah Penny and Jonathan Mills – your feedback has made this a better book.

I would also like to thank the people who keep me grounded and sane – Paul Ashton, Jonathan Mills, Maria Millman and Thao Dang. Thank you all so much.

Finally, thank you to my amazing Mum and Dad. You taught me to follow my dreams and to fight for what's important. I love you more than words can express.

The Author

Leigh Ashton is an author, speaker, trainer and coach. After a successful career in sales, Leigh founded The Sales Consultancy in 1995. Leigh had a principal mission: to rid the corporate sales sector of its old-school, increasingly outdated sales culture and, in its place, establish a people-focused culture to ensure better experiences and outcomes for both buyers and sellers. Specifically, the aim was to move away from a culture of ego-centric, fear-driven sales at any cost towards a people-centric Growth Mindset culture, where the salesperson's personal development is the key driver to increasing sales.

Leigh believes kindness and compassion is the foundation that springboards sales teams to greater success – knowing they have the support of their sales leader and the psychological safety to step out of their Comfort Zone to try new approaches. Also, Leigh promotes the need to learn from mistakes and receive feedback as a gift for personal growth and outstanding results.

Leigh has worked with global organisations such as Barclays, Harrods, NatWest, Motorpoint, Oracle, CDK, D-Link, British Airways, Volvo, Toshiba, AVEVA, Wright Medical, Stryker, Headspace and more. She helps organisations to build a healthy Sales Growth Mindset Culture that eliminates mediocre performance, boosts motivation and creates long-term sales success.

Leigh's mission continues to evolve, through researching thought leaders, business leaders, academics, spiritual leaders and psychology experts, and how these developments can grow sales and leadership success.

Find out more about Leigh and connect at:

🌐 www.sales-consultancy.com

in www.linkedin.com/in/leighashton1

🐦 https://twitter.com/LeighAshton247

Lightning Source UK Ltd.
Milton Keynes UK
UKHW021408190122
397397UK00007B/238